The Uncaged Voice

The Uncaged Voice

Stories by Writers in Exile

Edited by Keith Ross Leckie
With a foreword by Mary Jo Leddy

Cormorant Books

Canadian Heritage · Patrimoine canadien · Canada · Canada Council for the Arts · Conseil des arts du Canada · ONTARIO CREATES · ONTARIO CRÉATIF · ONTARIO ARTS COUNCIL · CONSEIL DES ARTS DE L'ONTARIO · an Ontario government agency · un organisme du gouvernement de l'Ontario · Ontario

We acknowledge financial support for our publishing activities: the Government of Canada,
through the Canada Book Fund and The Canada Council for the Arts; the Government
of Ontario, through the Ontario Arts Council, Ontario Creates, and the Ontario Book
Publishing Tax Credit. We acknowledge additional funding provided by the Government
of Ontario and the Ontario Arts Council to address the adverse effects of the novel
coronavirus pandemic.

LIBRARY AND ARCHIVES CANADA CATALOGUING IN PUBLICATION

Title: The uncaged voice : stories by writers in exile / edited by Keith Ross Leckie ;
with a foreword by Mary Jo Leddy.
Names: Leckie, Keith Ross, 1952- editor. | Leddy, Mary Jo, writer of foreword.
Description: Short stories and essays.
Identifiers: Canadiana (print) 20230442684 | Canadiana (ebook) 20230442730 |
ISBN 9781770867116 (softcover) | ISBN 9781770867123 (HTML)
Subjects: LCSH: Authors, Exiled—Canada. | LCSH: Canadian literature—21st century. |
CSH: Canadian literature (English)—21st century
Classification: LCC PS8235.E95 U53 2023 | DDC C810.8086/914—dc23

United States Library of Congress Control Number: 2023935165

Cover and interior text design: Marijke Friesen
Manufactured by Houghton Boston in Saskatoon, Saskatchewan in September, 2023.

Printed using paper from a responsible and sustainable resource,
including a mix of virgin fibres and recycled materials.

Printed and bound in Canada.

CORMORANT BOOKS INC.
260 ISHPADINAA (SPADINA) AVENUE, SUITE 502,
TKARONTO (TORONTO), ON M5T 2E4
www.cormorantbooks.com

Table of Contents

Introduction
by Keith Ross Leckie

THIRTY YEARS AGO, I had just moved into a house on a quiet, tree-lined street near High Park in Toronto with my wife and three young children. A few of our neighbours soon expressed their alarm that a refugee shelter was opening in one of the houses on the street just across from us. They imagined a bunch of impoverished, unsavoury foreigners lowering real estate values and bringing a rise in crime. One night just after the shelter had opened, a charismatic, blue-eyed woman in her late forties came to our door. Mary Jo Leddy invited my wife, Mary, and me to a special potluck dinner of celebration. A man, scarred and emaciated, who had spent four years in a brutal Eritrean prison for criticizing the government in print, had just arrived at the shelter to be reunited with his wife and five young children. A small handful of curious neighbours came over to meet them, and there was Eritrean food and music and dancing and joyful tears from the family of the prisoner who had been released. It was a life-changing evening for us.

Over the next few years as global conflicts flared up, there would be many other families coming to the Romero House refugee shelter on our street from Tibet or Burundi, Uganda or Colombia, then later Rwanda, Congo, and Kosovo, and later still, Iran, Eritrea and Mexico, Venezuela and Syria, and most recently Afghanistan, Kurdistan, Iran, and Ukraine. A vibrant community of friends and neighbours grew around the shelter. Mary Jo was able to buy three more houses in the neighbourhood to shelter the refugees with help from the Canadian Auto Workers Union, including a storefront office on Bloor Street. Mary Jo organized a system of young international volunteers to come and look after the growing number of families and, like Mary Jo, they would eat, sleep, and live in the houses with the newcomers. There were English lessons, pro bono lawyers, and refugee hearing tribunals with Romero friends in supportive attendance. There were food, furniture, and clothing drives. The Canadian Auto Workers Union donated a pickup truck. There were constant celebration parties like that first night with goats roasting on a spit and all manner of ethnic foods (or just pizza and chicken wings) and music. A lively street party on the third Saturday of June has run for twenty-seven years (excluding two COVID-19 years) with face painting and children's games, a dunk tank, a talent show on stage, and a banquet table featuring ethnic offerings from former refugees and food donated by dozens of local restaurants and grocery stores. And later, a street dance with a live band continues into the night.

Romero House has turned our street into a colourful community of involved neighbours. Each year, those original refugees from over twenty years ago return for the annual street party so they can see Mary Jo and honour what Romero House gave to them in the beginning. Many are now doctors, lawyers, scientists, and company owners. I have teared up when some of these former refugees have introduced me to their children.

One of the many offshoots of Romero House organized by Mary Jo Leddy was the Writers in Exile Supper Club, a casual, social, "bring some food and wine" kind of gathering of Canadian writers and former refugee writers. A few years later we became associated with PEN Canada through then-president Haroon Siddiqi. Out of this came many initiatives to encourage and assist former refugee writers, such as scholarships and internships at colleges and universities, access to translators, publishing options, and public readings. One small initiative was a workshop I organized where, once a month, translations of short stories, chapters from novels, and essays by former refugee writers were read and discussed. This led to the concept for a book, an anthology: ten refugee writers from ten different countries write ten pages each telling stories of why and how they had to leave their countries. That has expanded to fifteen writers — six women and nine men — from fourteen countries.

The stories in *The Uncaged Voice* can be brutal and heart-rending. These writers often suffered imprisonment and exile for years that can never be regained; some had parents die while they were unable to see them, others had children that grew up without them. We are asking much of these writers to go back and remember these often-terrible times and tell us about them. As Abdulrahman Matar says in his piece, after eight years of torture and starvation in a brutal Syrian prison for writing one article criticizing the government, "I want to leave everything behind me — the horrendous torture, the years without family or friends, the fear, the panic that haunts me — if only for one second." But he goes back to those memories for us, hoping to save future victims.

These stories reveal a terrifying new initiative by the governments of so many countries in the last few years — many of them once progressive democracies — to suppress the voices of their writers and artists. But these stories also show what is even more important to reveal: the strength, determination, and heroic resilience of human beings from all over the world to continue to seek truth, justice, and the freedom of expression.

KEITH has worked as a scriptwriter and novelist from his home base in Toronto. He lives with his wife — film, television, and musical producer Mary Young Leckie. They have three adult children. Keith has written many movies and miniseries for Canadian and American television. His latest novel in development, *The Good American*, is set in Afghanistan leading up to the tragic U.S. withdrawal.

Foreword
The Uncaged Voice

Mary Jo Leddy

FOR THE PAST thirty years or more I have lived with refugees ... and canaries in cages.

I have learned something about cages, real or imagined, and the people who inhabit them and the songs they sing.

I have learned from those who have shaken the bars, beaten the odds, and lived to tell the tale.

They have yelled and screamed and shaken the soul of memory.

Feathers lie in the bottom of the cage.

They have taught me to write real, to write wrongs.

I am still learning, still perched at the door of the cage.

There are others who share this perch, this perspective.

They sing, they say, that freedom is just beyond and beautiful, but one must beware because,

This is not a beautiful book. It is a terrible beauty. As the poet says.

These are the stories of people who rant and rage for freedom.

We need to hear these stories, the voices of suffering,

From the almost silent ones who have lost their feathers.

Still write with a feather dipped in bloody ink.

I know why the caged bird sings, as the poet says.

This book is a collection of stories from those whose voice is still between there and here.

They are the writers in exile of PEN Canada.
Perched at the door of the cage.
They pause and give us pause.

There is no period at the end of these stories.
These are stories of freedom, like the song of my canaries:

I can name these songs:
Hopi, *hope on one foot*
Bee Cee *Border Crossing*
Kurdi *the young boy who drowned in the Mediterranean*
There is little rhyme or rhythm to these stories, yet they sing along,
     like canaries
     who perch before the open door. Trembling.
Listen. They insist.
Persist. This is the price of freedom.

— *Mary Jo Leddy*,
"Easter, 1916," William Butler Yeats
I Know Why the Caged Bird Sings, Maya Angelou

Kiran Nazish
(Pakistan)

KIRAN NAZISH is a renowned international journalist who started her career in Pakistan and covered conflict and human rights around the world for two decades. She worked as a foreign correspondent covering all the post 9/11 wars, including in the Middle East and South Asia. Nazish founded and is the Director of the Coalition For Women In Journalism, a worldwide support organization for women and non-binary journalists.

INTRODUCTION

When people go missing in a country, stories go missing behind them. In a democracy, that is a sign of shattering. A rupture. These missing voices could in fact be the most telling story. And when journalists try to tell these stories in Pakistan, often they go missing as well, or worse, are murdered. Since Pakistan joined the so-called 'War on Terror,' an inherently troubled country saw a rise in missing persons and murdered journalists.

The Missing Equation

DEHYDRATED AND UNDER-SLEPT, I could barely concentrate on the frantic blur of this moment. Plotting the shutter speed of the camera to my subject's movement. Bowls of tabbouleh and clay-oven bread were tossed into the air from one side of the *dastarkhwan* (tablecloth) and caught on the other. I was interviewing the U.S. Kurdish militia fighters who had returned from the front line where they were fighting ISIS. They were exhausted from combat, likely jolly surprised they had survived, and they devoured their lamb kebabs like savages. Recently, I had been covering the rise of ISIS in Syria and Iraq and was currently documenting the siege of Kobanî when I started getting messages from Pushtun activists and journalists from back home. I kept ignoring the calls from the past; I didn't think my work could make any difference to the conflict. That past was more dangerous than being here, thousands of miles away in a different country. So here I was, mapping the rise of a new terrorist group, trying to understand how ISIS was growing so fast in this region. How did they commit horrific crimes and still recruit people? I badly wanted to make sense of it all. Why was terrorism metastasizing? What inflicted its followers?

What made people hate so hard that the anger saturated their humanity? I had asked very similar questions years ago back home in Pakistan.

It was not hard to chat with Kurdish fighters, the YPG, and the Peshmerga, who were very willing to speak. They burst into juicy stories and, as a journalist, I found talking to them much more productive than what I'd experienced back home where, after months of relationship-building, sources were still afraid to speak on the record.

The Kurdish fighters were here to liberate Kobanî — a small town bordering Turkey and Syria — where ISIS was raging on. My colleagues and I, working for western media, were covering this conflict from a few kilometres away on the Turkish side of the border. There were enough journalists reporting the story that this spot came to be known as the "media hill." Clearly, my sources here were easier to speak to on the record because they were on the side of history the media could cover without facing the stifling pressure of censorship. This was a war where you knew who the enemy was. We were reporting from well-defined borders. For journalists, the dangers were very real. Not long before this time, my colleagues James Foley and Steven Sotloff had been kidnapped and beheaded by ISIS.

The threats were not invisible. You knew who the enemy was. When I'd worked in Pakistan's much more muddy waters, the threat came from the state — the very institution that is supposed to be guardian and protector of foreign journalists who face threats like terrorist kidnapping or other risks.

Here in Kobanî, as a militia commander shared details of the fight, I scribbled in my notebook amidst an almost deafening echo of *Ser chava ser sera* — Kurdish greetings said aloud for the fighters in praise of their bravery. Every cheer made the fighters blush with pride. Such was the air of valour; I had witnessed it before, many, many times in my own country.

Big players on the global stage were rooting for these fighters to defeat ISIS, and that meant we, as journalists, had the freedom we needed to tell the story. So here I was, doing what I was supposed to do: "tell the story."

As my translator walked towards me, he yelled, "Your phone is ringing again," and handed me the device. I stepped outside in the sun, eyes squinted, and looked at my phone to see a dozen missed calls and messages from Pushtun friends, including from the veteran journalist Sailab Mehsud. I braced myself and read a few messages. There were familiar pleas in 'minglish' (English, mingled with words of Urdu or the other way around). I had been getting similar messages for a while now. "We need someone to speak for us"; "IUDs are killing the children"; "fake military operation"; "they (Taliban) are escorting the streets"; and "we are sick of the army."

Some asked if I "could find another journalist" who could look into the story, since I couldn't. The Pushtuns were frustrated by the information black hole in the country, which, on top of the oppression, violence, displacement, and war was adding to the trauma of the Pushtun community in and around Waziristan. This region had been called "the treacherous tribal region of Pakistan" by the international media too many times and for a reason. I had been asking other journalists in the country to meet some of my sources because a) I was working as a foreign correspondent in a completely different region and b) I was afraid of getting myself into trouble again.

Pakistani media was too censored to utter a word — journalists have been killed for doing this in the past, and the choice was either censor or face death — let alone ask hard questions about the military establishment's full-fledged involvement in sheltering terrorists while pretending to quell militant groups. Many Afghan journalists and officials criticized Pakistan for sending terrorists across the border, but no international power wanted to make Pakistan accountable — not even the United States, which had spent billions of dollars to fight this so-called war on terror. Once, in 2013, in an interview I did with a NATO leader in Kabul, I asked about the organization's stance, and they responded, "We believe Pakistan is doing their best." This was, in fact, a statement identical to what was being said by any international leadership whose military was stationed in Afghanistan. I had asked a similar question to U.S. and UK leadership and had received responses that bestrewed the criticism many in Afghanistan were raising about Pakistan's uninterrupted support of terrorist groups. Global leaders needed Pakistan's cooperation as they prepared to pull out of Afghanistan, so they continued to give a free hand to Pakistan no matter how many innocent people lost their lives or how many civilians were displaced. After all, the U.S. was not itself free of moral wrongdoing. Hundreds of innocent civilians — mostly Pushtun from the same region — had been killed by U.S. drone strikes.

Pakistan was against the drone strikes, but not because innocent Pushtuns were losing their lives. Rather, the military establishment was losing allies in the terrorists and offshoot groups they were supporting. While civilians were being killed, the drones were even more successful in killing terrorists, and over the years accuracy had improved. All the major terrorist leaders in the Haqqani Network, the Taliban, and Al-Qaeda were taken out by drones — not the Pakistani military. The natives of Waziristan warned that the Pakistani military was working in tandem with the terrorists. They were witness to the cooperation between these parties, and for years before leaving Pakistan I was told stories from the region about various forms of abuse by the military. These stories were strictly silenced by the military: journalists could not report them. The press was even barred from interviewing locals, and a complete media blackout of this region thrived. Journalists found in the region were threatened — I was one of them — and if they dared to ask questions they were killed.

Some parts of Pakistan's porous border with Afghanistan had been blocked not only to journalists but also to civilians from these regions. Under the garb of so-called military operations against terrorist groups, the Pakistani state had evacuated millions of Pushtun civilians from Waziristan — a region that has been called treacherous by many western correspondents, and a place I had written about in the *New York Times* during my tenure at the paper. The trouble was, there was much that had not been written. The cloak of secrecy that the Pakistani state had wanted was working.

Besides, the world's focus had shifted to the fight with ISIS. There was no appetite to hear more about the Taliban and Al-Qaeda, even if they continued setting off bombs in Afghanistan and Pakistan. As the global gaze was evaporating, Pakistan cracked down on dissent even harder. Activists went missing, while journalists regularly received threats and were occasionally abducted. Pakistani media called this area the "no go zone."

The last time a colleague wrote about it, his bloated body wound up floating in a sewage canal near the country's capital. A former colleague and friend, Saleem Shahzad, was killed for connecting the dots between Pakistani military and terrorist groups — a story no journalist has dared to write about since. Not long before this, Nasrullah Afridi was blown up in a car in Peshawar, the capital city of the North-West Frontier Province. A military official once smirked at a lunch, "Guess he didn't learn his lesson." He reminded me of Hayatullah Khan, who was abducted by the military back in December 2005, tortured from skin to bone, and then found dead six months later. It sent reverberations among all journalists in the tribal areas. The war against the press had reached a pinnacle. Killing journalists had become so common that it was spoken about openly, even to other journalists. Still, as a woman, and one who worked for foreign media and had somewhat influential friends globally, I thought I was safe under the many layers of protection.

According to Reporters Without Borders (RSF: Reporters sans frontières), the Committee to Protect Journalists (CPJ), and the Coalition For Women In Journalism (CFWIJ), Pakistan is one of the deadliest countries for journalists, with between two and four killed every year. That said, murders are not the only way journalism is killed in the country. Pakistan's most notorious Inter-Services Intelligence agency — the ISI — targets the press in multitudes of ways.

I had come to Kobanî to stay away from that chaos. Too many of my friends, mentors, brave journalists, and activists had either been killed or targeted in horrific ways in Pakistan. My sources were threatened for talking to me. And my own homeland remained the most dangerous of all places for me, even though in my career I have covered many other dangerous beats and regions, whether it was the conflict in Iraq, or Assad's bombing in Syria, or the cartels in Mexico. I never felt more confronted with invisible threats than I did in Pakistan. Perhaps, as foreign correspondents, we can leave foreign lands and go back home, but what does one do when the war is in the home, and the enemy is the caretaker of that home?

I looked at my phone again and excavated a number of messages from the past few days. I had similar desperate messages from Manzoor Pashteen, a young veterinary student who had formed a small volunteer group with friends. Between studies and exam deadlines, he was working with fellow student volunteers to gather aid for the Internally Displaced Persons (IDPs), from Waziristan. The internally displaced from South and North Waziristan were now at the mercy of a small group of student volunteers because the Pakistani government was not able to attend to many of their needs, for safety and survival. Millions of dollars in aid that came in U.S. dollars was certainly not being spent efficiently on the real victims of the U.S. 'War on Terror.'

Often Manzoor and many other sources would say, "The money is spent to feed the militants, not civilian victims."

In the years to come, Manzoor Pashteen would rise as an unlikely leader — a type of Nelson Mandela in the region — first cheered and praised by the Pushtuns in the country and later by the rest of the nation. Later Manzoor's movement would animate support from global activists and from the Afghan leadership, including Ashraf Ghani and Hamid Karzai. Manzoor's call for accountability for the victims of Pakistani military operation would garner support from American intellectuals like Barnett Rubin among others, and instigate a new wave of cross-border activism demanding an end to Pakistan's atrocities. Former Canadian diplomat Chris Alexander was one of those who used some of Manzoor's revelations and started the #SanctionPakistan campaign. But most importantly, Manzoor Pashteen united a nation in conflict with itself, a nation caught in the delicate dance between victimhood and warrior.

For decades, the Pakistani military had harassed ethnic communities, often separately in different parts of the country. The built-up anger from that harassment of the Pushtun, the Baloch, the Sindhi, the Mohajir — tens of thousands from each ethnic community went missing or were murdered — all would culminate in 2018, when different groups came together to support Mazoor Pashteen's Pashtun Tahafuz Movement (PTM).

Years later, everyone would relate to the call and demands of Manzoor Pashteen and a movement he began for the reconciliation and justice of those oppressed and mistreated by the Pakistani military under the so-called 'War on Terror.' While the majority of their people were innocent victims of U.S. drone strikes, they were also the first and most frequent target of every terrorist group that existed in the region, from the Tehreek-e-Taliban Pakistan, to Al-Qaeda, to offshoots of these groups.

Sometimes, it blew my mind to ponder how much suffering was possible. Here I was covering yet another terrorist group, so obnoxious and appalling in its calibre that it made the Taliban and Al-Qaeda seem tame. *Astaghfirullah*!

I wiped silent tears on the back of the truck. My translator's "Are you okay?" kept echoing as we drove to our hotel in the city, two hours away from the border.

Was I okay? Well, I felt like I was being pulled in two directions. I felt my conscience calling upon me. Surely, being here on the border with Syria was important, but there were many more journalists here to tell the story. Meanwhile, the international media was barely interested in Pakistan beyond the terrorism and foreign policy angle. And local media at home had been silent, which was understandable given the threats faced by journalists.

These calls and messages were affecting me. People in my country were getting hurt. Censorship and misinformation back home were taking innocent lives. Activists and journalists were stifled and threatened, while some disappeared, as did anyone who would speak on their behalf. The Mehsud tribe in particular were being persecuted and killed. Extrajudicial killings of Pushtuns were rising. Children were being killed or injured by landmines the Pakistani military did not bother to clear for civilians, and millions were displaced. And most importantly — a repetition of a trend that had happened in other provinces — people were going missing. This wasn't good news because when people went missing in Pakistan it often meant irrecoverably horrible things were happening.

This moment was important for me; it pulled me back to the place I came from and was running away from. I felt that I hadn't only been running away for my safety and sanity, but that I had been running from duty. After perpetual and repeated censorship, you desperately welcome any form of freedom. I thought running would liberate me, instead it was burdening. I felt wounded. I felt like a captive to guilt. What do they call it? Moral injury. It squeaked my bones. My homeland had taught me the values I carried everywhere I went in the world: to be courageous in the face of fear, to uphold the values of equality and equity, to make the powerful accountable in the darkest places and times. Power through light. Root for democracy. I realized I shouldn't run.

Therefore, much to the credit of all those courageous and unhindered activists, I went back to work again in Pakistan and picked up a story I had buried after receiving a direct and indirect threat. I was quite aware that I could face threats again, but I thought covering other more visibly dangerous conflicts in the world had prepared me better for the challenges in my own country.

The tenderness of treacherous lands is such that it pulls you back.

Cradle of Civilization — Where the Bloodbath Began

Welcome to the warm, ravenous shores of Karachi, one of the most populated, polluted, and spectacular places in the world. Here, nostalgia is comprised of walking on the Sea View beach on the edge of the city; it feels like the breeze is always in sync with your mood. I am not sure if you know, but something you can't find anywhere else in the world is the aromatic street *biryani* that one could eat out of a plastic bag, the sultry, marshmallowy version of red meat submerged in thick curry, called *nihari*. The moment it lands in your mouth, your entire body is captivated.

The port city, where global trade connects the Arabian Sea to the subcontinent, has for centuries attracted big players in the region for opportunities. These are the shores where the Umayyad dynasty invaded a mass of land that is now split into three countries: India, Pakistan, and Bangladesh. Centuries ago, the Saudi warrior general Muhammad bin Qasim conquered Sindh and Punjab at the age of seventeen. Thus began the spread of Islam and Muslim rule in the region under the Mughal Empire. Eventually, the Brits were attracted by the flourishing of a trade economy, arts, and culture, much of which we still enjoy in the region between what is now the divided India and Pakistan. This led to the eventual ousting of the Mughal Empire by the East India Company, which subsequently became the British Raj.

I come from this country. It's a land where humanity dates back long before any of these invasions. Sindh, the province that holds the stunning metropolis of Karachi, has been called the cradle of civilization by many historians. It was the centre of ancient Indus Valley civilization, which itself was one of humanity's oldest cultures, having flourished between 3300 and 1750 BCE, rivalling civilizations in Egypt and Mesopotamia in size and sophistication. Modern-day Pakistanis who live here are descendants of a permanent human settlement that dates back to about 7000 BCE. In the sixth century BCE, Sindh became a Persian province, and in 326 BCE it was conquered by Alexander the Great. In the ensuing centuries, Buddhist Greco-Bactrians, Scythians, Persians, and Rajputs held sway in the region. How is that for heritage?

I come from the country where the great Himalayas and Karakoram meet, in the land of Hindu Kush in the north, home of one of the world's greatest glaciers and some of humanity's oldest indigenous groups, such as the Hunza people, who for centuries have lived here. I come from a country where music can be made on tin cans, and cricket can be played on swirling, dusty streets. Cars passing by have to manoeuvre around wickets made with crates that once held bottles of Pepsi Cola and avoid running over the player who shouts at the top of his lungs, *chakka* (goal). I come from a country where cricket champions are made on the uneven roads.

I come from the country of one of humanity's greatest stoic philanthropists, Abdul Sattar Edhi, who himself lived very simply while he ran the biggest networks of ambulances, orphanages, shelters, schools, and other humanitarian resources greater than the government could ever match. He was nominated for the Nobel Peace Prize multiple times but never won, which offended many Pakistanis who had been inspired by the impact of his work, especially during natural disasters, where his foundation saved millions of lives. He also sent aid in times of disaster around the world.

Once I asked him how he felt to be overlooked by the Nobel committees. He put his hand on my shoulder and said, "Awards don't matter to me, service does."

In a country riveted by sectarian, religious, and political violence, Edhi famously said, "My religion is humanity." Every penny in the Edhi Foundation is donated by the poor and middle class of Pakistan. And although many have aspired to be humanitarians on the level of Edhi, I have yet to find any who compare to him for the impact of such pure good, untouched by politics or religion, anywhere else in the world. If anyone doubts this statement, they should dig deeper into Edhi's work.

I come from a pauperized country where people work very hard and die very young. My grandparents, who in my memory seemed to have lived long lives, actually died of ill health in their early sixties. My youngest brother was born under a curfew, the memory of which perhaps would never leave my body.

One afternoon, wild skirmishes broke out between the Rangers (a military battalion imposed to enforce a curfew) and political workers for the Muttahida Qaumi Movement (or MQM). The sound of gunfire was piercing the air, and bullets entered our fourth-floor apartment at Al-Karam Square, making holes in the walls. Next morning, a sort of ceasefire emerged, and we quickly packed a small bag, mainly filled with baby supplies, and snuck out of the building to head to a neighbourhood where relatives lived and there were no skirmishes. The new "safer" neighbourhood was called Golimar, which literally means "pull the trigger." Did someone say safe neighbourhood?

The skirmishes weren't widely covered on national television, and I heard my grandparents wondering out loud whether their parents, who migrated amidst bloodshed from India to Pakistan in 1947, would think it was worth it. "If we die here, we will die in our home," my grandparents whispered in the echo of open fire. "Was this worth the sacrifice our parents made for a new country?"

When I was growing up here in the 90s, political violence was in full swing. On a monotonous day, we could confuse the sound of a rickshaw passing by with the sound of gunfire. That's how often we heard

Kalashnikovs in the middle of Karimabad, a neighbourhood unilaterally ruled by a somewhat newly formed political party called MQM. This party represented the Mohajirs — immigrants — who had taken the journey from India during the partition of 1947 and settled in empty homes in the then capital of Pakistan, Karachi. The Mohajirs felt left out by the resident parties like Pakistan Peoples Party (or PPP), chaired by Benazir Bhutto, and Pakistan Muslim League-Noon (or PML-N), representing the Punjabis and chaired by Nawaz Sharif. The MQM especially became more prominent during a time, in the 80s, when the Pakistani military wanted to try something other than the infamous coup to oust democratically elected leaders, namely the above.

The fighting, helicopters hovering over the apartment building, the bloodshed, the Rangers with bulletproof vehicles were scary, but what I remember most is feeling awful for my younger siblings who couldn't play because it was unsafe to spend much time outside. And when we did go outdoors, if my mum needed to breastfeed our youngest brother, we would surround them to make a human shield, as if our tiny bodies could handle the bullets.

I often saw dead bodies being carried through the back streets. In our neighbourhood, every other home had a dead son in the near past, or near future.

Most people in the country who had a TV set watched one channel: the Pakistan Television Corporation Network (PTV), a state channel. There was no private TV and no independent news. But the media did not cover these stories widely, if at all. Sometimes hundreds of young boys in our neighbourhood were killed, and the national television channel would give a one-minute bulletin. The fact that most people in the country did not see how deeply and regularly we were suffering made us feel even more left out.

In fact, parts of the 90s and early 2000s in Karachi saw phases of notorious bloodbath. I don't remember the year exactly, but once I remember going to a hospital looking for a relative's body. We got a phone call. He'd been killed in a shootout. When we arrived, we found so much blood on the floor of a ward that it reached our ankles. These two decades

were also embellished with some of the most gruesome reports of missing
and murdered people. At one point in the early 2000s in Karachi, at least
twelve people were killed daily, in waves of targeted violence, often in
daylight. A few neighbourhoods were particularly ravaged by the violence
and often residents would get text messages revealing the location of a
"body in a bag" found nearby. The victims were political activists who
were first picked up by thugs, tortured in custody, and then murdered and
mutilated. Their bodies, often filled with bullet holes, were then thrown in
different corners of the province. The goal was to create fear and silence
amongst the Karachiites in these neighbourhoods. All of this violence was
perpetuated by MQM and its faction, who had been supported by the military establishment in the early 90s, to disrupt democratically elected governments, including those of Benazir Bhutto and Nawaz Sharif.

The only place as dangerous as Karachi in this era would be Mexico
or Colombia at a time when cartels were rife. And the reason I believe this
was not so widely known is definitely because of the censorship in Pakistan. Journalists who reported these stories were regularly threatened, and
often killed themselves.

It was only occasionally that violence in Karachi made the international news, but often attention came after death, destruction, and irreplace-
able hurt. Avoidable violence. When the world caught up with us, it was
already too little, too late.

Imagine the circumstances of a society going through this. Imagine regular shootouts in residential neighbourhoods. Sometimes my mum sent
me to fetch milk from the milkman, who kept his shutters down to avoid
being targeted. (It was a common role for children to be sent to pick up
milk or bread, as they are more nimble than adults and can more easily
run away if spotted by Rangers or thugs.) I would have to knock on the
shutter and say my name to get a bag of milk — he had to know who had
come or he wouldn't open the shutter. On my way back, I would walk
sneakily through the back streets.

From this very young age, I knew what I wanted to do in life: tell the
stories no one was allowed to tell. I learned to be invincible in dangerous
places, develop the instinct to use my petite body and brilliant mind to

help navigate an environment that could get someone killed, and come out of there as someone useful. I had been trained to be the journalist I would become later on in my life.

The So-Called War on Terror of the U.S. and the Death Squads of Balochistan

It was rare that the Karachi Press Club was not bustling with interesting people. I was still a teenager, and perhaps the youngest in a cohort of English newspaper employees who visited here often. This was the ground zero for the misfits of the media, as well as underpaid, underappreciated, and often invisible local-language press reporters and photojournalists. We came here when we wanted to have a conversation outside of the newsroom's leaky corridors and stayed longer for the addictive *karak chai* (thick, dark, overcooked tea) and the cheapest *biryani*. A few summers earlier, I had gotten my foot into the door of *Dawn* newspaper as an intern and was blown away by my luck walking into the great Zubeida Mustafa in the corridors, not to mention often being invited by "Fieca," the venerable Pakistani political cartoonist, into his office to shadow his work. My summer internship turned into what would become my lifelong career.

In 2002, when *Wall Street Journal* writer Daniel Pearl was tragically and grossly murdered by terrorists, it sent shock waves amongst all of us journalists in Pakistan. We were already well aware of the dangers the Pakistani media faced — abductions by the intelligence agencies, torture and murder by political parties like the MQM. But such a gruesome murder of a foreign journalist — and one we had deep respect for — was a message to journalists in our homeland and those who came from the rest of world. The very fact that a foreign journalist could be killed by a terrorist group in this country was symbolic of the increased danger local journalists felt. The word *danger* for journalists had crossed a line, and we immediately knew many more of us would be next.

After 9/11 happened, Pakistan under General Pervez Musharraf was coerced into supporting for the 'War on Terror' launched by President Bush. At the time, the United States allied with a government ruled by the military, an institution that had interrupted the country's democratic process from the very start, often by coups that ousted elected leaders or by other means, for example supporting thug groups like the MQM in Karachi.

Not long after the September 11 attacks in the United States, the Americans invaded Afghanistan in the hunt for Osama bin Laden. Pakistan was the primary U.S. ally in the 'War on Terror,' and hence, the province of Balochistan became a key staging ground for military efforts. Much of the land served as a major military transit route for the United States and international forces. Trucks and supplies were transported from the seaport to Afghanistan, and intel was shared back and forth through land interlocutors as well as technology. General Musharraf also made a part of Balochistan available to the U.S. as the base for drone operations.

U.S. dollars flowed in to bolster Pakistan's efforts to help the 'War on Terror,' aiding contractors and the trucking industry, and new businesses emerged. And yet, despite these benefits, the citizens themselves, the people who lived on the land where this was happening, were excluded. Eventually, Baloch people started speaking out.

Baloch are an ethnic tribe with a centuries-old history and heritage and have long resided in this land called Balochistan. Yet they had always felt neglected, first by the Brits during the British Raj, and then by Pakistan after the Indo-Pakistani partition in 1947. When they saw the military and its allies benefiting from the boom of resources being used throughout their land, they knew it was their right to demand a share for basic needs. But when they raised questions and demanded resources for their schools, hospitals, and university, they started getting abducted. The culprits were a new group of thugs famously supported by the Pakistani military and intelligence agencies, and commonly known in Balochistan as the 'Death Squads.' Pretty self-explanatory, for the Baloch people their name was not a noun, it was a verb. Just like in the 90s in Karachi, with the abductions and disappearances of activists, students, and political workers by the MQM, now the Baloch started disappearing, though the Death Squads in Balochistan were vicious. They abducted activists and students from their homes and tortured them with gruesome cruelty, often for months and years. During my reporting, I spoke to dozens of Baloch families whose loved ones were returned with "body in the bag" similarity: their bodies were often thrown in the corners of random parts of the city, and in most cases the bodies showed clear signs of torture, including burn marks and bullet holes.

Indeed, most regional journalists were too afraid to cover the story due to safety concerns, but those who did got threats. Even Pakistani journalists from outside Balochistan feared reporting there and were tracked by Pakistani intelligence. Balochistan was a 'no-go zone.' Every time I visited the province I was followed and approached by intelligence agencies who warned me to "not write anything." Even when I went to cover a humanitarian disaster, like the Awaran earthquake, I got a knock at the door of my hotel by the infamous Inter-Service Intelligence (ISI). When I did continue reporting on Balochistan, I received serious threats. Some of the victims and sources I interviewed were told they would face "consequences" if they spoke to me again. These threats to my sources were sufficient for me to be silenced, and one of the primary reasons why I decided to cover other parts of the region like India, Afghanistan, and Nepal and stay away from any coverage in Pakistan.

Between 2009 and 2012, the situation got so out of hand that hundreds of activists, scholars, and others started disappearing and no journalist was allowed to report on the missing and murdered Baloch people in local media. Press clubs and student unions were forcibly shut down. A colleague from the *New York Times*, Carlotta Gall, who was one of the rare foreign correspondents to go to Quetta, the capital city of Balochistan province, was physically harassed by the ISI. In the following years, no foreign journalists have been able to enter the region independently. Some have gone embedded with the Pakistani military, which basically doesn't count. As of 2021, according to many Baloch activists, since General Pervez Musharraf joined the alliance supporting the War on Terror, between 55,000 to 70,000 people have gone missing from Balochistan.

Whether they have made the news or not, disappearances in Pakistan's Balochistan province have never really taken a rest. Even today, every week several Baloch persons go missing, and even today the media in Pakistan and outside the country do not diligently report on the issue, if they do at all. Baloch activists and journalists are not only killed inside Pakistan, but possibly also outside the country. In 2020, Baloch journalist and scholar Sajid Hussain went missing in the Netherlands and was found dead in a river in Uppsala, Sweden. In December of that year, my friend Karima Baloch — an exiled Baloch activist and a former source back in Pakistan days — went missing in Toronto. The next day, her body was found in the water, similar to how Sajid was found, causing global outrage and horror amongst exiled Pakistanis. A CBC Radio investigation series called *The Kill List* reveals the circumstances and backstory of Karima's mysterious death and why many, including myself, believe she was killed by the Pakistani ISI.

A short return, and the final word

The calls I had gotten while covering the siege of Kobanî, from Pushtun activists like Manzoor Pashteen and veteran journalists like Sailab Mehsud, got me on an airplane. I had acquired a commission from a New York-based publication and was hoping to finally dig back into this story I had left behind many years ago — partly because several journalists had been killed connecting the dots between Pakistani military and terrorist groups. But I felt by this time, late 2014, there had been sufficient criticism and revelations about the Pakistani military's involvement with terrorist groups that I was less likely to be excluded as a troublemaker in the eyes of the military establishment or intelligence agencies. I always travelled with local residents when I went to the tribal region of the northwest frontier that bordered Afghanistan because it gave me protection to enter without being traced by agencies. As necessary, I wore a burqa that shields a woman's body and face, and this allowed me to travel in the region for many years without being detected. I often also travelled with tribal leaders who were kind enough to be my shield. Even though I was not a Pushtun, they trusted me, mostly due to the relationships I had developed over many years.

This was the first time I had travelled in Pakistan since 2012, when I did so without a burqa and more openly. Imran Khan had invited an

American antiwar activist group, Code Pink, to a rally to Waziristan, where they called for an end to U.S. drone strikes. Eventually, the rally was blocked from entering Waziristan by the Pakistani military, and even locals from the area were not allowed to enter. Why? Many Waziris told me the reason was "Pakistani military is hiding terrorists in our home." That year I had tried covering this story but received death threats while I was still researching and interviewing residents from the region.

This time, when I returned to the northwest, I had better arrangements. This reporting trip started with tragedies right off the bat. On the first day I arrived in Peshawar, the capital city of the North-West Frontier region. I was taken by some sources to a location where two dead bodies had been found, blood-soaked and mutilated. The young men had bullet holes and torture marks on their bodies, similar to what I had seen back in Balochistan and a long time ago in Karachi. These young men had disappeared several weeks before, after raising questions about the Pakistani military continuing their support of terrorists. The respected veteran Sailab Mehsud later added details about his own witness. I was told by over a dozen sources, including Sailab, that the recent anti-terrorist operations by the Pakistani military were fake and that, in fact, the Pakistani military themselves were killing civilians and local Waziris in Waziristan and counting those civilian killings as terrorist fatalities. A dozen sources, including Manzoor Pashteen, told me that the Pakistani military was conducting mass abductions of innocent civilians who had raised their voices against Pakistan's fake military operations. I met families whose sons, fathers, and grandfathers were tortured in front of their neighbours to teach a lesson to the community. This was a silencing tactic, and, in the absence of cellphones and any communication service, the only way information could get out was through those few who were able to get through the barricades and Pakistani military guards.

During this trip I spent months speaking to people, travelling from town to town in areas that were not under the military's control, from D. I. Khan to Tank, to Bannu and Mohmand — all different corners of the North-West Frontier region bordering Afghanistan. I recorded hundreds of hours of interviews and acquired dozens of images and video evidence from sources. As usual, I was able to travel with the help of wonderful and courageous regional activists and journalists, but this time things were more precarious than in previous years, which I became acutely aware of when I learned someone had tipped off my location and itinerary to the intelligence bureau. One afternoon in February 2015, my translator, source, and myself were stopped as we were trying to sneak into Waziristan's outskirts on Mir Ali road. The result was a long detention filled with threats, the beating of my translator, and confiscation of our equipment and phone. This was followed by another series of troubles that haunted me for many years after. Eventually, I was escorted by intelligence officers all the way back to the capital of the country, Islamabad, and was told I would regret publishing anything of what had happened. My translator was kept and tortured for several days, creating fear and anger in his community. Over a dozen of my sources were contacted and threatened for speaking to journalists, which told me I had been followed and tracked for quite some time. I faced several other consequences I cannot mention here for the safety of others.

Needless to say, amidst warnings, death threats, and visits from the intelligence agency I dropped the story and left the country. Fortunately, I had a work engagement to leave for in Hong Kong, which helped me wrap up quickly enough, as I feared the probability of an intelligence agent contacting me was escalating. I fear if I had not left, I might not be alive today. Even though at the time I was simply afraid for the safety of several people who had worked with me, and even though I wanted to disengage, months later, outside the country, it all sank in. My own life had been in very real danger. This realization caused the trauma to kick in in a debilitating way. After a series of panic attacks and severe depression during my time between Iraq and New York, I ended up in the hospital several times due to total collapse. A trauma that sort of paralyzed me, and it took years of work and treatment to recover.

In any event, once I was out and safe, I continued my work for years to come and went on to report from Iraq, Syria, Mexico, and many other places. Eventually, a few years later, Manzoor Pashteen launched an organized campaign revealing all the atrocities the Pakistani military had been committing for more than a decade in Waziristan and other Pashtun areas — not only that they were harbouring terrorists, but that they continued to send militant groups into Afghanistan while targeting innocent civilians in our own country. Manzoor's activism led to the formation of a political party that now holds a seat in the parliament, represents those who are oppressed across the country, and regularly — amidst threats and violence — demands accountability. Their members are frequently put behind bars, but these activists continue to challenge an institution that has destroyed the fabric of Pakistan's democracy.

What really helped me the most in my healing was doing useful things. I spent years studying neuroscience and enrolled in courses at MIT to understand trauma and the human brain. It helped me make sense of both pain and human beings. Simultaneously, I built an organization that supports and advocates for women journalists who face violence and persecution from the state, often amidst very little support. Called the Coalition for Women in Journalism, we are now a global organization that monitors press freedom violations against women and 2SLGBTQ+ journalists from 128 countries, and our advocacy work has supported hundreds of journalists in times of crisis. Before our work, there was no database of press-freedom attacks on women journalists. Our work has led to journalists being released from prison or relocated to safer places. During the recent fall of Afghanistan to the Taliban, we evacuated more than four hundred Afghani women journalists and their families, and have continued similar support for Ukrainian, Iranian, Egyptian, and Turkish-Kurdish women journalists in times of crisis.

I was lucky to have left Pakistan at a time of danger myself. Every day, I am aware that many of my journalist colleagues who face similar threats cannot simply leave. Some don't even want to leave the country that is close to their heart. Many of my courageous friends back home continue to work amidst threats because they are fearless and committed. The courage to speak and illuminate the dark corners is bigger than the fear of being killed or silenced.

The moment we remove free speech, a nation loses its freedom. Freedom of speech, and freedom of movement are *the missing equation* in a broken democracy. And as long as we have fearless journalists who take risks to tell the truth, and who try to strengthen this community, we can have some hope.

Aaron Berhane
(Eritrea)

AARON BERHANE was the founder and editor-in-chief of the largest independent newspaper in the violent dictatorship of Eritrea. When the government ordered a crackdown on journalists, Aaron saw a dozen of his friends and colleagues arrested and imprisoned without legal recourse or medical aid. All are still in prison or dead. He was able to escape across the border into Sudan under a hail of bullets from border guards and eventually arrived in Canada. Aaron founded *Meftih*, a newspaper for the Eritrean community in Canada, campaigned for his fellow journalists who were still imprisoned in Eritrea, completed a master's degree at Ryerson University, became a professor at George Brown College, and was leader of the Writers-in-Exile Committee of PEN Canada. On May 1, 2021, Aaron suddenly, tragically passed away from COVID-19 at the age of fifty-one, leaving behind his wife and three children.

INTRODUCTION

After one hundred years of colonization by Italy, Britain, and Ethiopia, Eritrea won its independence in 1991 and formed a democratically elected government under President Isaias Afwerki in 1994. This government, unfortunately, became increasingly oppressive, arresting opposition leaders, banning future elections, and, in 2001, shutting down all independent newspapers and imprisoning the journalists.

The Tattoo on My Brain

SOME MEMORIES ARE seared in your mind like a tattoo on your skin. They float on top of your thoughts whenever something triggers them. Tuesday, September 18, 2001, is one of those memories. I remember everything that happened on that day — the day the regime banned my newspaper.

It was seven a.m. on an ordinary day in Asmara, Eritrea. My brain was still reshuffling the information I had gathered about the attacks on the World Trade Center a week earlier. I had written an article on it for the next issue of *Setit*, the twice-weekly newspaper of which I was editor-in-chief. I was in bed when my wife turned on the radio to listen to the morning news.

"Starting today, September 18, 2001, the government is ordering all private presses to stop their publications." The disturbing words of the announcer of Dimtsi Hafash Radio, the government station, froze my train of thought. The official statement accused us of violating press laws and ignoring the warnings they had given us. I felt as if I'd had a bad dream. I couldn't move my head. I lay still under the blanket.

"Did you hear that? This is a total lie," my wife said. "Why do they do that? We don't deserve that."

She was right! The hard-working journalists as well as the people who benefitted from the newspapers didn't deserve that after the huge sacrifice they had made to liberate the country from one hundred years of colonial rule by Italy, Britain, and Ethiopia.

I remembered the cheerful spirit of the people when we celebrated our independence in May 1991; when the press law was issued in 1996; when I launched the first independent newspaper in the country in 1997; the stories we covered, the interviews we made; the collaborative work I did with all independent newspapers; the noise we made on behalf of the people; then the closure of the newspapers. In a few split seconds I saw the birth, growth, and then death of my newspaper like a series of snapshots.

I got up and dressed, picked up the keys of my Toyota Land Cruiser from the drawer, and drove. *Setit* was distributed on Tuesdays and Fridays. I thought the government would have confiscated the copies before they left the printing house, but, luckily, my paper had already hit the market before they got a chance. I saw the last edition of my newspaper being sold on the street as I drove downtown and uptown through Asmara. *Setit* had been the first independent newspaper to circulate in the streets and it became the last to be seen in those same streets.

In one day, the business that had taken us years to build had been closed by a simple stroke of a pen from a paranoid president. I thought about the impact of such an unjustified decision on the democracy of the country that had just started to flourish and its impact on more than 1,500 people who would lose their jobs. I thought about the children who supported their parents and themselves by selling the independent newspapers, and I thought about the employees who worked at the printing house and the newspapers. The hopes and dreams I had of seeing the establishment of a democratic government in the country all evaporated at once. I felt an unimaginable grief. I did not understand where this attack would hit next.

I parked the car near Bar Folia to place a call to my sources from a public phone. I was told the breaking news that had not been reported by Radio Dimtsi Hafash: the government had arrested eleven of the fifteen senior officials who had written an open letter that criticized the president. I had published this letter in *Setit*. My sources advised me to watch my back and alerted me to how volatile the situation was. It was then that I realized there was no turning back for the regime.

A few hours later I drove to my office. I found the staff of my newspaper sitting in the front yard debating that morning's developments. Fesseha Yohnnes — the oldest member of our staff and a talented writer — was optimistic, as were younger members such as Dawit Isaak.

"They just shut us down because they don't want us to write about the jailed senior officials," Fesseha said. "They will let us continue our work once they settle the issue."

I did not believe that, but I hoped he was right.

Around noon I met with Matewos Habteab, editor of *Meqaleh* newspaper and Amanuel Asrat, editor of *Zemen* newspaper at Rendez-Vous, a café near Cinema Roma, a relic of Italian colonial art deco architecture. We were friends and had strengthened our friendships while we were enrolled at the University of Asmara. Matewos and Amanuel had also been great contributors to my newspaper before they had launched their own. Now we were confronted with the most critical moment of our young journalistic careers. We needed each other's advice more than ever before.

As Matewos and I drank tea and Amanuel sipped an espresso macchiato, we agreed to take extra precautions and resolved to write a letter to the Ministry of Information condemning the false accusations against us and demanding clarifications about the specific reasons for the government's decision to close our newspapers.

Three others joined us and also signed the letter: Medhanie Haile, deputy editor of *Keste-Debena*; Yusuf Mohamed Ali, editor of *Tsigenay*; and Said Abdelkader, editor of *Admas*. At the end, Amanuel and I handed the letter to the Ministry of Information on September 21, 2001. I didn't know I would never see those talented and dedicated editors again.

Besides the editors, a number of journalists were arrested soon after. I was one of a few who evaded arrest because we were not home when the security agents came to our houses. Many of my colleagues and my inspirations were not so lucky: Seyoum Tsehaye, a gifted photographer and writer; Dawit Isaak, a brilliant writer and author; Fesseha Yohannes (Joshua), a talented playwright; Dawit Habtemichael, a deputy editor of

Mekalih; and Temesgen Gebreyesus were among those thrown in jail. According to several sources, seven of the journalists who were arrested have since died in prison, and no one knows about the rest. That's heartbreaking.

Sometimes, I even wonder how we survived the four years that led up to the shutdown of the presses. The intention of the government had been very clear right from our beginning in 1997: they didn't want the new independent presses to succeed. They tried to systematically weaken us by denying our access to information, ignoring our requests for interviews, and refusing to give us permission to establish a journalists' union. Once we started to control the agenda of day-to-day discussions, the government began using telephone threats, physical threats, and intimidation to silence us.

Whenever I remember September 18, 2001, I see how much we lost as a country and as a people. The journalists we lost were dedicated and ambitious and could have contributed a lot to Eritrean society. Some of them were parents with a desire to see their children grow, graduate, and get married; and some of them were young and were planning to start families. Unfortunately, the Eritrean dictator took away that opportunity from them.

As I write this, they have been held incommunicado without trial or fair justice for nineteen years. This has been a huge burden for me and other colleagues who escaped the grip of the regime. Advocating for the release of those imprisoned is my priority; increasing awareness about their situation is my obligation. Sadly, despite the collaboration of organizations that advocate for freedom of speech and human rights, we haven't managed to get the results we have wanted.

Occasionally, I wonder how to remember this day. I have contradictory feelings. On one hand, I feel the pain of my colleagues who have languished in prison for no apparent reason apart from the fact that they are journalists, and on the other hand I feel relief for escaping the grip of the dictatorial regime. It was a lucky day for me, but an unlucky day for my colleagues. Nevertheless, I have never stopped thinking about them, and I will keep reminding others to think about them too, not only on this day but every day, as it is etched on my brain like a tattoo.

Chapter 1 — Farewell

(Excerpt from *Burden of Exile* by Aaron Berhane)

It was around one a.m. when I heard the sound of a car pull up beside the compound. Its engine cut out. I slipped out of the room I'd been pacing in and went to the gate to see who had arrived. I lay flat on the ground and peered through a gap between the iron gatepost and the concrete wall that surrounded the compound. From this vantage point it wasn't possible to see the car or the people inside it, but I could discern the voices of two people, a man and a woman.

Were they lovers stealing away in this desolate part of Mai-Chihot, a district on the outskirts of Asmara, or something much worse?

I strained to see further and was able to make out a small car, a Fiat 600 that was parked in front of the gate, but I still couldn't see the people inside it. I crept to the other side of the gate but could see no better from there. All I heard were unintelligible voices. Were there more than two people in the car? Had they finally come for me?

It was the night of January 6, 2002, and I had been in hiding in this remote part of Asmara for 103 days. That night was meant to be my last in the country. Arrangements had been made for me to steal across the border to Sudan and elude the government agents who were pursuing me.

The house I was staying in belonged to a relative. It was only partially built, like many of the houses in Mai-Chihot. The main house, a type of villa, consisted of three bedrooms, a large living room, two bathrooms, and a kitchen. There was also an outbuilding that contained two small rooms plus a bathroom and a modest kitchen — the only rooms in the compound that were fully finished. My makeshift bedroom was outfitted with a single bed and a small table. The other room was a storage room accessible through a door in my bedroom. It was piled with bags of cement, cans of paint, and stacks of broken tile. In the event that someone came into the compound, I'd made a hiding spot for myself between the bags of cement. A high concrete wall separated my compound from the neighbouring houses. An iron gate, much taller than a man and wide enough to admit a car, faced the street.

I was the only person living in the neighbourhood.

That night, I was waiting for my cousin Petros to arrive and take me to say my final farewell to my wife and children. Petros was one of the few people with whom I had contact while I was in hiding. He was over six feet tall but walked with a stoop, and that, along with his bald head, made him seem older than his thirty-two years. When circumstances dictated, he could disguise himself as an old man by draping a shroud about his shoulders and walking with a cane. He was my connection with the outside world and took me out to meet with my sources, the people who could smuggle me out of the country or forge false papers.

When Petros would come to see me, he always parked seven hundred metres from the compound so as not to draw any attention to my location. This is why I was sure that whoever it was in the Fiat, it wasn't Petros. To calm myself, I told myself that the people in the car were there by chance and weren't interested in me. But it did no good. I felt restless and feared that my escape plan had been foiled.

In the living room of the villa, I had left the backpack I had prepared for my escape. I slipped inside the villa and shouldered my pack. I wasn't sure what I should do next. I opened the back door of the villa so that I could easily cover the few metres to the outbuilding and my hiding place in the dusty storage room. If the people outside did try to breach the compound, I took some small comfort in that they would at least be slowed down by the shards of glass that protruded from the top of the wall. This delay would grant me a few precious seconds to reach my hiding place.

The engine of the car came to life and the headlights turned on. I had my face pressed up against the bars of a glass-less window and I startled at the sound of the engine and the bright lights. I retreated several steps and gripped the straps of my bag tightly. Headlight beams shot through the gate and seemed to rake across the vacant yard. The car backed up in line with the gate. It struck me that perhaps they intended to drive straight through the gate. The engine kept running and the sharp smell of petrol wafted across the yard. My pulse raced, and my breath came rapidly. I wanted to run to the storage room while also wanting to see precisely who had come for me. I remained by the window, feeling the coldness of the night and listening the rumbling of the Fiat's engine. Then, with a lurch, the car was thrown into gear, and it pulled away.

Once the Fiat had gone, I took my backpack off and set it down on the floor. My heart was still racing, and I sat on the steps at the rear of the villa to be soothed by the night's chill.

I startled when I heard a pebble land in the front yard. I sprang to my feet and primed myself for whatever might come next. A second pebble landed. I stole along the wall and peeked through the gap between it and the iron gate. I saw Petros's familiar shape.

"Did you see the car?" I asked Petros.

"Yes, I was waiting for it to leave," he said.

I opened the gate to allow him in and shut it behind him.

"Did you see their faces?" I asked.

"No, but I don't think we have anything to worry about. If they tried to chase us with a Fiat 600 you could outrun them on foot," he laughed. "Everything is clear now. Let's go."

"What took you so long?" I asked, trying to read his expression.

"I had to wait until the maid left," said Petros holding the door for me. "Your wife wanted her to finish washing clothes before the water was cut off."

"Oh, I see, today is Friday," I said. The authorities distributed water to different areas of the city on different days, but it didn't flow all day even on the designated days. It was one of the main complaints we used to hear from people whenever we went to cover stories. Despite that, the availability of water never seemed to be a high priority for the government.

The moon was full and lit our way. Apart from some dogs scavenging through a pile of garbage beside Petros's car, nothing else stirred. We climbed into the car and drove along the narrow, unpaved roads of Mai-Chihot. The street lamps that lined the road were dark. We crossed street after street before we reached a paved road that led to the centre of Asmara.

Asmara looked peaceful, especially now that the soldiers who had menaced the population for months had withdrawn. They had been deployed in September 2001 when the authorities cracked down on the press and arrested rival politicians. The office buildings glowed with the diffuse yellow light of the street lamps. They flitted between the palm trees that lined the boulevards and gave the impression of a sharp couple heading out on a date. I felt obliged to commit to memory these last impressions of my city before I left it, my family, and everyone I loved.

Petros was driving fast past Fiat Tagliero, Gejeret, Bar-Jima, Godaif, and Kahawta while checking the rear-view mirror to see if we were being followed. I had the window open and was enjoying the feel of the wind blowing through the beard I had grown over my months in hiding.

"No one will recognize you with your long beard, including your wife," Petros said.

I looked at my face in the side mirror. I was thirty-two, but the beard made me look much older.

Petros slowed down to turn onto my street. My heart beat faster as we got closer to my house. The streetlights were on, and the streets were starkly lit so that you could see a person from half a kilometre away. Petros parked the car and surveyed the street before crossing the one hundred metres to my house. We were the only people out.

Petros knocked on the gate twice while I watched anxiously to see if anyone was following us.

My wife appeared and unlocked the gate. "Mielat, my love," I whispered. I stepped inside and drew her to me. Petros took a last look at the street before locking the gate behind him.

We crossed the yard that fronted my house. Frieta's bicycle and Mussie's toys — a helicopter, a car, and soccer balls — were scattered in the yard. Petros remained in the yard as a sentry while I went inside the house, holding my wife's hand. I led us to the children's bedroom where I found all three of them sleeping peacefully. Frieta, my beautiful, energetic eight-year-old daughter, the boss of the house, lay diagonally across her bed, her blanket bunched up around her feet. Mussie, my chubby four-year-old, slept on his belly, and Evan, still only six months old, lay in his cradle. I watched them and listened to the sounds of their breathing. I wondered if I would ever see them again or if they too would have to be raised without a father, as I had been. What a miserable legacy that would be.

I kissed my children on their foreheads, careful not to wake them. My eyes filled with tears, and I averted my face so my wife wouldn't see. She, however, did not conceal her tears from me. She stood by Evan's cradle, watching me kiss our children, her tears streaming down.

"Do you think we will see each other again?"

I put my left hand on her shoulder and wiped her tears with my right.

"Yes, Mielat. I will reunite us in a peaceful country."

"I don't know, Aaron," she said and looked up to meet my eyes. "If they catch you while you're trying to escape, the punishment will be worse. Isn't it better to stay in your hiding place for a while longer? Things may change."

We had discussed this topic whenever she came to visit me in my hiding place. My wife is very persistent; she returns to an issue until she gets the answer she wants. But this time the matter was settled.

"Mielat," I said, "my hiding place will not remain secret for long. The security agents are still sniffing around after me, but I have great people who will help me escape. Don't worry. I'm sure I will make it."

The truth was that I didn't know if I would make it or not. The dangers were many. But for my wife's sake, I projected confidence. I held her in my arms and gazed at her.

"You remember how I escaped from the Ethiopian soldiers in Kisad Molekseyto? You know how fast I can run."

"That's different, my love," she cried. "This is more dangerous. They have distributed your picture at every checkpoint. They will catch you before you even reach to the border with Sudan."

Petros interrupted. "Come," he said.

I followed him outside and told Mielat to stay where she was. Through the fence we saw a green military vehicle parked near Petros's Land Cruiser.

"They just came?" I asked.

"Yes, just now. No one has left the car yet," Petros said.

The full moon and the street lights allowed us to see what was going on. Two soldiers came out of the car with a small ladder and rested it against the wall of my neighbour's house. They climbed over the wall and dropped down into the compound.

"Does that family have a son or daughter who might be evading national service?" Petros asked.

My neighbours' four children lived abroad, and they didn't have anyone in the national service. I didn't know why the soldiers had targeted their house. Petros and I watched to see what would happen. After about five minutes, the gate opened, and the soldiers came out leading a young man in handcuffs.

"Do you know him?" Petros asked.

"I don't think so. He could be a relative hiding himself from the hunters like I have been." I put myself in the poor man's shoes and felt terrible. "Someone must have betrayed him," I said.

The soldiers drove off quickly and disappeared from sight. I was gripped with apprehension. What were the chances that I too would be betrayed by the people who had promised to help me? None of them were being paid. They were doing it because they believed in me as the editor-in-chief of our country's first independent newspaper who had tried to bring freedom and change to our country. They were ready to sacrifice themselves to save my life. I had no choice but to trust them.

"We should go," Petros said.

I went back inside my house. Mielat was still standing in the children's room, gazing upon them as if she were seeing them for the first time. Tears still streamed from her eyes. They landed on her pink pyjamas and left dark splotches. I stood next to her, embraced her, and cast a final look at my children. Mielat buried her head in my chest and sobbed. After a time, she calmed down, and I kissed her lips softly.

"I have to go now, Mielat," I said. "Please, be strong, and believe we will meet again."

We held each other tightly.

"Please, tell our kids how much I love them," I said.

She nodded silently.

Petros returned. "We should go, Aaron. It's almost three a.m."

Mielat grabbed me again and kissed me fiercely. "I love you very much.

Don't forget us, please. You have to survive for us, for your children," she said and released me.

I fought back my own tears and followed Petros towards the gate, Mielat trailing after us. In the yard, I picked up Frieta's bicycle and leaned it gently against the wall. Then Petros and I went through the gate and hurried into his car.

From Chapter 6

Ahead of us, the terrain was flat, and we could see the light of Kassala, Sudan. No compass would be needed once we crossed the border. Had it been possible to drive, the trip would have taken an hour. But it was more like eight on foot across the desert, through sinking sand and acacia trees with half-inch thorns.

Samson led the way; I walked second and Gebray followed me. Due to the thickness of the bushes near the valley, we had to squeeze between them to get through. Sometimes the thorns would catch onto our clothing so badly that it would take time to extricate ourselves. It was worse, of course, when they snagged on our skin. We couldn't cry out in pain or make any sounds, but rather struggled with the thorns as quietly as we could. Samson stopped us whenever he detected any hint of movement. Most of the sounds came from wild animals — rabbits, snakes, foxes, and hyenas. We were on their turf, and we couldn't complain when they startled us by darting out of their cover. But my biggest fear wasn't the animals.

After we walked for about thirty-five minutes, Samson stopped. He told us quietly to show more caution as we got closer to the border. I emptied the sand from my *shida* sandals and adjusted them on my feet. Despite all my efforts to break in my *shida* while I was in my hiding location, they were already causing me discomfort.

Samson waited until both of us cleared the sand from our shoes. He pulled up the sleeves on his shirt and checked his watch.

"It's almost eleven thirty: the army must have left by now, but you can never be too careful."

He stepped forward. Both Gebray and I followed him. We penetrated the bushes one after the other by clearing the spiderwebs that clung to our eyes and mouths. Sometimes, we had to contort ourselves sideways to find a path through the dense, prickly growth. Since the bushes were only a few feet high, we also had to hunch down when we neared the border. I trusted Samson and his knowledge of the region and felt confident that he was leading us in the right direction. Eventually, we reached the border and Samson stopped beside the thick acacia trees that stood about five feet high.

"This is it," he said.

There was no border fence. The line of the border was represented by small hills that we could see from afar. While he explained to us what was Sudan and what was Eritrea, harsh voices roared at us from seemingly every direction.

"Stop where you are!" I heard the clatter of guns mixed in with their shouting.

They were only a few steps away from us. I couldn't believe everything had fallen apart so drastically. Samson had done his best to get the latest information, but unfortunately, he'd been wrong. The army hadn't left the area at the appointed time, and we were trapped.

I didn't see any option but to make a mad dash towards Sudan. I charged ahead into the thick acacia. Adrenaline suffused my body and as I ran like man possessed, with a speed I'd never thought myself capable of. Gebray and Samson charged along behind me. When the soldiers realized we weren't going to surrender, they started firing their guns. I thought my life would end right there, bloodied by bullets and thorns on the flat land of the border. The border of life and death.

The shooting broke open the silent night. Rabbits jumped out of their holes, foxes out of the bushes. By scattering in all directions, they drew some of the fire of the soldiers away from me. We were all of us running to save our lives. The shooting kept up and bullets whistled over my head. However, it never occurred to me to surrender. I knew that if I was captured, it would be the end for me anyway. So, I forced myself to run, to prolong my life for even one second more.

The night was pitch-dark and it was nearly impossible to see what lay before me. I weaved in and out of the bushes. I had to break the branches that barred my path, wrench myself out of the grip of the thorny bushes that seized my skin and clothes. But nothing could stop me. Mortal fear made me capable of superhuman feats. I flew until I stumbled over a downed tree and dropped to the ground. My body and my bag went in opposite directions. I didn't bother collecting my bag but just kept going, leaving my belongings behind. I needed to get away and stay alive. I heard Mielat's words in my head.

"You have to survive for your children, for us. I don't want to be a widow. I don't want to raise our children by myself. Remember the dream we had to get old together; to see our children grow, graduate, and start life of their own."

I felt my mother's prayer too. She petitioned all the saints and God himself to protect me from those who would wish to take my life.

I ran this way for over an hour. I was deep into Sudan by then. I had escaped. I finally slowed down and took my bearings and gathered my thoughts. I kept hearing gunfire from where I had last seen Gebray and Samson. I checked myself. It felt like there was no part of my body that hadn't been torn. My face, arms, legs, and belly were stained with blood and sweat. There was blood on my right leg and below my T-shirt, which felt like a more serious injury. If I'd been shot, I didn't feel any grave pain. But the blood that flowed from my leg worried me. I carefully diagnosed my injury.

"I'm all right. It's only a scratch."

I scooped some soil from the ground and sprinkled it onto the wound to staunch the bleeding. I stretched my back and looked around. I heard the barking of dogs ahead of me and gunfire in the distance behind me. Finally, the shooting stopped. I didn't know what it meant, but I hoped both Gebray and Samson had also managed to get away. I felt a hollow, lonely pang in my stomach. I kept going to Kassala, Sudan, hoping that Gebray and I would find each other there.

Savithri
(India)

SAVITHRI is a freelance journalist and author with a passion for writing about politics and exposing human rights violations. She is currently a Ph.D. student in English Philosophy at the University of Barcelona. Savithri grew up in Kerala, a southwestern coastal state in India. After suffering for years in an arranged, abusive marriage, she left the country in 2010, unable to adapt to the patriarchal tendencies and conservatism of Indian society. In Barcelona, Savithri is active in the Indian publishing sector as a translator, columnist, and novelist.

You Slayed My Wings!
You Really Did!

"PLEASE, LET ME do this!"

I raised my teary eyes to my mother. She was sitting in a chair, listening to my plea. As an English teacher, she was always keen on displaying a teacher's discipline and rigour in front of her children.

"We don't have money." My mother said it in a voice she didn't even believe.

"Amma, I don't like to wear gold. We can sell these bangles." It was my last string of hope.

"Stop this nonsense!" Her face reddened with anger. "You are twenty-one. It's time to search for a suitable groom. We need to save for dowry and ornaments."

"But you promised me!" I cried aloud. "You promised that if I could get a master's degree in literature, I would be allowed to study any course I wanted."

"Yes! We did! But that was the only option to make you study what we wanted. It is over! If you want to continue, try to join a teachers' training centre. We don't want a journalist in this family."

"You cheated me! Liars!"

I couldn't stop myself. My mother left the room, leaving me to adapt to the fact that all I had ever wanted was just a dream.

My father came into the room to see if the problem was over.

"You promised me!" I shouted. Tears were rolling down my cheeks. With a triumphant laugh, my father slammed the door against me.

I felt cheated. It was my long-cherished dream to be a journalist who travels around the world, who covers war fronts, who writes about poverty, inequality, and injustice. Little did I know that my parents, who saw their daughter spreading her wings to fly away, were sharpening their knives to cut them off. They wanted me to be a teacher, just like my cousins. They wanted their daughter to have education, but only the courses that they approved. Education of their choice, job of their choice, groom of their choice, and a life of their choice!

All this happened twenty-four years ago, but I still remember the gleam of that smirk on my father's face. They mercilessly dragged my life in all the ways they wanted. They arranged my marriage to someone I had never met. He was uneducated and was working as a driver in a Gulf country. My parents' only concern was his family and financial status. They had money. My parents married me to him without inquiring about his character or his behaviour where he lived and worked.

My subsequent life was hell. The only responsibilities I had in that house were to make heirs for the family, do all the kitchen chores, and satisfy my husband's needs at night. He made me pregnant twice, regardless of my permission or wish. I lived in that house for four years as a slave or housemaid who didn't even have the right to look at a piece of newspaper. My husband had many illicit relationships in the country where he worked. His relationship with a married woman became public and he was forced to take responsibility for her and their daughter due to threats from her family. He decided that the only way to do that was to leave his three-year-old child and me, his legal wife, who was eight months pregnant with our second at the time. He threw his wife and two children out of his life like a torn old shirt and married that woman.

Most interesting was the reaction of my parents, who had forced me into this marriage without my permission. My children and I became a burden to them. Due to the unbearable humiliation of having a divorced daughter at home, they unleashed physical and mental abuse on me. I left home with my children when it was alleged that my younger sister was not getting suitable marriage proposals due to the disgrace I had caused to my family.

I found a small job and started living with my children in a faraway city. We were very happy there because there was not even a shadow of my family or the villagers who were laughing at me. Soon I got a job in a bank. I could provide good education, good food, and good living conditions to my children. Still, my family's hatred for me was not over. They made sure that I was not present at any of the family's auspicious ceremonies. I was equally disturbed by the discrimination I felt when I had to say in public that I was divorced. Slowly I came to the conclusion that it would be better to leave the country for a peaceful future for me and my children. Seven years after my divorce, I had the opportunity to get over the walls society had built around me. Without even thinking what my parents or the community would say, I fled the country to a bright and happy life.

Such an escape from India would have been impossible for even one in a million women at that time. The invisible nets of tradition and patriarchy are so powerful that nobody can fly away easily. What intimidated my parents was the word 'journalism,' a career that did not conform to the patriarchal values that their society cherishes. The stories of other girls who wanted to enter similar careers at that period were no different from mine. Despite these circumstances, some female stars shone in the field of journalism, inspiring girls. As time went on, girls began to fight against the system, wanting to follow in the brave footsteps of their predecessors.

Journalism was considered as a masculine career at that time. Society had divided careers on the basis of gender, and families had forced girls to choose feminine careers like teacher, nurse, and administrator instead of jobs conventionally allotted for men, like journalist, legal practitioner, executive and so on. There were a number of brilliant women journalists working in English as well as in the vernacular press at that time, but still society considered the mainstream media a world incompatible for girls.

I was born a day before the Emergency — a period in which Indira Gandhi declared a state of emergency across India. In addition to the restrictions imposed on civil liberties, the government also shackled the activities of media. Although radio and television were under their control, the government imposed censorship to control the print press, who were the only remaining independent media. The print media initially protested in despair for losing their freedom, but eventually had no choice but to submit to the inevitable. Against the expectation of the Indian public regarding free, uncorrupted, and unrestrained media, journalists chose to crawl when they were asked to bend. But by the end of the Emergency period, which lasted twenty-one months, the Indian press had made a comeback like the world had never seen before. Many women journalists came on the scene as part of that uprising. I belonged to a generation that grew up reading these women and listening to their heroics. Beyond the tedious careers determined by the family, we coveted the bright and exciting world of media. The world of news, which was completely uncertain about what would happen the next moment, fascinated me.

Although India's status was that of a democratic country, my childhood was a time when state terrorism was rampant. Journalists believed that it was their responsibility to extract the truth from the remnants of the Emergency. For the first time since independence, news reports from India began to catch the world's attention. As the public interest in credible news increased, a new awakening took place in the media and, as a result, many new publications appeared. This pluralism in the media helped people to observe things from different angles and it enabled democracy to function more efficiently. The emergency period sparked new excitement among journalists to detect corruption, question authoritarian tendencies, and call the truth out loud. Their interest in reporting international news stories also became greater. Investments in the media resulted in increased advertising revenue. Encouragement of common people, who were eager to have information, made journalism a better profession and strengthened the role of journalists as watchdogs in society. This new revival in the media attracted many talented women to the field.

Female journalists like Anita Pratap, Seema Guha, Ritu Sarin, and others started reporting fearlessly from hotspots like Punjab, Kashmir, the northeast states of India, and Sri Lanka. They broke all precedents of masculinity in the media sector with exclusive features from war zones and interviews with militant leaders. Following the issues between Sri Lankan Tamils and Sinhalese, Anita Pratap travelled several times to Sri Lanka, which was a dangerous conflict zone at that time. She was the first journalist to interview the LTTE leader Veluppillai Prabhakaran. In 1997, while working as the South Asian bureau chief of CNN, she won the George Polk Award for reporting the Taliban takeover of Afghanistan. I still remember cutting out a picture from the newspaper of her with a big smile on her face and pasting it on the door of my closet.

The sincerity and commitment of the women journalists from the 80s brought them fame and recognition. Seema Mustafa's articles from conflict zones in India and war fronts in foreign locations like Beirut are milestones in the history of the Indian media. She managed to creep into Beirut in disguise and stayed there for three weeks, reporting the war. As the only Indian media person reporting from the war-torn city, Seema attracted national attention.

Neera Chaudhary was awarded the People's Union for Civil Liberties (PUCL) Journalism for Human Rights award for her investigative reports on forced child labour, the Maya Tyagi gang rape case, and children's hardships in Tihar Jail. Sheela Barse, a freelance journalist based in Bombay, wrote a series of articles on child prostitution and the condition of women in brothels; her work resulted in court action. She also won the PUCL award for reporting the sufferings of female prisoners in Indian jails.

Several women journalists, such as Tavleen Singh, Saraswati Ghosh, and Ritu Sarin, gained recognition for political reporting in both English and vernacular languages. Sincerity to their work and commitment to society have brought about many changes in the socio-political life of the country. As a result of increased women's representation in media, by the end of the 80s, women's issues had grown in importance and visibility. As a consequence, the presence of magazines for women and covering issues of specific concern to women increased tremendously in the market. *Eve's Weekly* was the most prominent among these magazines, in comparison with others like *Femina* and *Women's Era*.

During this period, the determination of a brilliant journalist, Chitra Subramaniam, had a major impact on the 1989 elections. Subramaniam exposed the Bofors scandal, which involved Prime Minister Rajiv Gandhi and many other government officials and politicians in India and Sweden. Unable to withstand strong pressure from the government, *The Hindu* newspaper stopped publishing her articles. Instead of retreating, Chitra continued to release information through the *Indian Express* and *The Statesman*. The strong evidence brought out by Chitra tarnished the image of Rajiv Gandhi as an honest politician, and as a result, brought about the fall of the ruling party, the Indian National Congress.

Until this time, news about women's issues was appearing in local newspapers only, when there were major issues at the national level. In the state of Kerala, where female literacy was highest, the mainstream media was reluctant to employ women. A study by Gita Aravumudan, published in 1987, found that *Malayala Manorama*, the most popular daily newspaper in the state of Kerala with a circulation of over 650,000, was not employing women. But, in the form of magazines for women, the ripples of change slowly began to appear in the vernacular languages as well. *Baya* in Marati, *Sangharsh* in Hindi, *Nari Mukti* in Gujarati, and *Ardha Akash* in Assamese are some examples.

Unfortunately, most of these feminist publications did not have the ability to compete with the major newspapers that were already entrenched in the market. Many of them got financially distressed by the lack of sponsors and advertisements and disappeared slowly with the economic reforms implemented by Prime Minister Narasimha Rao, a representative of extreme right-wing politics who came to power in 1991. He silently witnessed the growth of the Bharatiya Janata Party — which had emerged as a replacement for the Indian National Congress — and the BJP-led demolition of the Babri Masjid mosque. These developments resulted in the Hindu-Muslim conflict that the country is experiencing today and steered Indian society back to the ancient and outdated values of the patriarchy.

Many girls entered the field of journalism during this period, excited by the brilliant performances of women journalists of the past decade. As these girls became women, they relentlessly advanced into covering such areas as foreign affairs, crime, politics, finance, human rights, and sports, which had been handled mainly by men. But the gender discrimination that existed in media houses made it difficult for women to enter and survive in the field. Most male editors and senior journalists behaved with the presumption that women could not spend enough time on work due to family responsibilities. The general perception in the media was that very few women could perform like their male counterparts as they had to deal with the demanding roles of wife and mother. Such patriarchs did not hesitate to find pleasure in rumours that these women were using their femininity to achieve goals they had worked hard to attain. These stories stimulated the patriarchal community, which enthusiastically spread the word that media houses were chaotic places where women could not work. In this context, journalists like Shoma A. Chatterji began to speak out about such injustices as the fact that women journalists who dealt with women's issues were only given the opportunity to do so on Sundays. Following this, the *Times of India* started a column on weekdays about women achievers, but it did not last long.

There was a growing tendency to exclude women journalists from serious news stories. Stories by women journalists about serious topics were often dismissed without due recognition, regardless of the hard work behind them. Most of the time, senior journalists assigned their female colleagues to trivial subjects such as entertainment and fashion, which did not require much intellectual work. This attitude towards female colleagues was also reflected in the news on women's issues.

More than local dailies, English newspapers and magazines focused on women's problems like rape, dowry deaths, female foeticide, and political issues like the Shah Bano case. The growing competition for advertisements among women's magazines in the late 1980s was also a major factor in simplifying the content. Gradually, the goal of every publication has become getting more readers and thereby attracting more advertisers rather than providing quality content. The media, which had been satisfying the intellectual needs of readers and enabling them to raise questions, shifted their attention to addressing transient and ephemeral human curiosities. Consumerism, as in all other spheres of society, has intensified the discrimination suffered by women in media. Although investors who entered the media after the Emergency period caused a new impetus in early days, the devaluation caused by the conversion of publications into a consumer product also affected women journalists tremendously.

After 1990, India slowly entered the world economy by easing import policies and welcoming foreign consumer goods to the market. The media also stepped into the emerging capitalist system and consumerism in order to protect their own interests as commercial enterprises. As a result, due to the abundance of opportunities in the media, many women entered the field. Women started occupying senior positions like executive editor, joint editor, resident editor, and political editor. Indian media also witnessed women like Anjali Mathur and Amrita Shah becoming editors of men's magazines. These enthusiastic women had no hesitation in dealing with "hard news." In newspapers like *Statesman*, *The Hindu*, *The Hindustan Times* and *The Times of India*, women started becoming prominent in areas dominated by men.

After my divorce in 2003, my desire to continue my studies took off, but I did not have time to pursue my dreams as we badly needed some income to live on. At the same time, the nature of the media was also changing. The media started evolving from being the third eye of the society to a corporate, revenue-oriented business. As media is primarily a commercial enterprise to make money for the owner, editors were forced to turn to stories that increased the sales of their publications. They were compelled to include simple stories that satisfied people's basic emotions, rather than serious stories of an investigative nature. Many media houses began to marginalize women by assigning them trivial stories. Meanwhile, a new threat to women emerged with the rise of Hindutva.

Hindutva is a fascist, violent ideology founded by V.D. Savarkar during the colonial period. Savarkar, who opposed Gandhiji's non-violent methods of struggle, was also charged but acquitted as one of the conspirators in his assassination. Savarkar's successors communicated with Hitler and met Mussolini to acquire ideas to shape the ideology of the Bharatiya Janata Party. Women journalists, along with many female artists, filmmakers, activists, and academics, were subjected to increasing violence due to the influence of Hindutva. Many were verbally and physically assaulted while doing their work and some were killed. The BJP is now the strongest and most popular among the organizations under the label of Hindutva. Dissenting voices against their sectarian ideas are dealt with by lynching, riots, bombings, threats of rape, unjust imprisonment, and so on. The experience of Rana Ayyub, who tried to disclose the political conspiracy behind the Gujarat Riots, is an example.

According to official figures, the 2002 Gujarat Riots resulted in the deaths of 254 Hindus and 790 Muslims. According to the *Citizens' Tribunal Report*, nearly 2,000 people were killed, several women were raped, and assets were destroyed. Through sting operations in 2010, Rana Ayyub reported on the nexus between the military intelligence and the extremist Hindu organizations behind the riots. Her evidence points to the involvement of the current prime minister of India, Narendra Modi, and the BJP's president, Amit Shah. Based on the evidence gathered, Rana Ayyub wrote the book *Gujarat Files: Anatomy of a Cover Up* and subsequently faced many hardships. She was subjected to threats of gang rape, murder, slut-shaming, and humiliations from Hindu extremists in social media for doing her job efficiently. Pornographic videos with her face Photoshopped in have spread across the internet and have included her address and personal phone number. Eventually, the UN Human Rights Office had to put pressure on the Indian authorities to take action to end the hate campaign against Rana Ayyub.

Growing intolerance and aggression against dissent has now become an unhealthy characteristic of Indian society. Those who attempt to report impartially against injustice face fascist-minded backlash, because in one way or another they are hurting someone's ulterior motives. This change in society stems from a regime that has moved away from pluralism and has promoted religious extremism, patriarchy, and authoritarianism. India has become a dangerous country for journalists who do not submit to the interests of the state, as evidenced by the assassination of Gauri Lankesh.

Gauri wrote an article protesting the extrajudicial killings known as The Encounters in India. She intended to publish the article in her family-owned newspaper. The story covered the death of her old classmate turned Maoist, Saket Rajan.

Gauri's brother, Indrajith Lankesh, was a BJP supporter who claimed that Narendra Modi was the inspiration in his life. He was adamant that Gauri not publish the article and forced her to withdraw it by pointing a revolver at her head.

After this incident, Gauri left the newspaper and started her own venture, *Gauri Lankesh Patrike*. Gauri wanted to make a difference in society through journalism. Her criticism of the government grew stronger. Gauri argued that a lasting solution to the Maoist problem should be found through negotiations, rather than using violent means to quell dissenting voices.

Gauri published Rana Ayub's book, *Gujarat Files*, in Kannada, and that bold initiative increased the government's hatred for her. As part of a conspiracy to stifle anti-Hindu voices across the country, Gauri Lankesh was shot dead in front of her house in 2017.

But Gauri was far from the only woman facing punishment and threats. The most respected and prominent person in the Indian Women's Press Corps, seventy-five-year-old Mrinal Pande, was charged with sedition in January 2021 for her tweet regarding the farmers' protest in India. In the same month, someone broke into the house of journalist Neha Dixit. More recently, someone has been following her and making threats of rape, murder, and acid attack over the phone.

The threats faced by women journalists belonging to the Muslim community are much scarier than all these. Most are facing daily threats of murder and rape through their social media accounts. Journalists like Arfa Khanum Sherwani complain about the problems they face as journalists, as women of their own opinion, and as women with Muslim identity. These issues are constant, frightening, and destabilizing for them. In April 2020, Masrat Zahra, the winner of the International Women's Media Foundation's prestigious Courage in Photojournalism Award, was accused of trying to mislead the youth and destroy the peace in society by posting anti-national posts with criminal intent. She was charged under the Unlawful Activities Prevention Act (UAPA). Under this law, the police have the power to detain individuals without any special charges or bail.

It is alarming that most of the social media accounts that are threatening and humiliating women belong to BJP activists who claim that the prime minister is their hero. The police are reluctant to register criminal charges against these accounts, which are operating according to the Hindutva agenda. This trend has become strongly entrenched in the country. According to the annual Reporters Without Borders' World Press Index, India ranks 142nd in press freedom, falling below neighbouring countries Nepal, Bhutan, and Sri Lanka. This report makes it clear that the threats of the nationalists, who are exponents of Hindutva, become destructive and deadly when their target is women.

India is not rushing towards progress under the regime of Narendra Modi. Instead, it is going back to the male-dominated, outdated customs, the horrific caste system, and toxic nationalism that existed centuries ago. Unless proper action is taken against attacks on media, freedom of expression, and women's voices, such tendencies will be normalized, and dissenting voices of democracy will be silenced. Parents and society will continue to deter today's girls from becoming journalists, and the growing religious and political threats against empowered women will go unchecked.

Abdulrahman Matar
(Syria)

ABDULRAHMAN MATAR is a Canadian/Syrian journalist, novelist, and poet. He has written five books. He has been a political detainee five times for his opinions and writings critical of government policies. Abdulrahman is a member of PEN Canada and the Writers in Exile collective. He is a member of the Board of the Syrian Writers Association and managing editor of *Awraq* magazine.

He is the founder and director of the Syrian Mediterranean Cultural Forum — Toronto. It is a cultural forum concerned with introducing Arab and Mediterranean creators residing in Canada and their various literary and artistic works to Canadian society. The Forum has organized important cultural events across Ontario.

Abdulrahman is the winner of the Empowering Communities Award: Commitment to the Arts, Multicultural Festival / Toronto 2021.

The Road to Freedom:
Arrest, Fear, Displacement

"WELCOME TO CANADA," said the judge, with a serious face but a hidden smile.

Or that is how it appeared to me.

I can only attempt to explain how I felt when her words entered my ears, passing through my chest. The phrase ended twenty years of fear, arrests, prison, pursuits, and homelessness. I felt like I was in a misty space, and for a moment, I was transformed My being was restored: my complete existence, with all my human rights. And no one could violate those rights anymore.

In my native country of Syria, 'welcome' has a different meaning. It means to be arrested on a charge of having an opinion and exercising freedom of speech. It means undergoing extreme torture, possibly until death.

In June 2012, an intelligence officer said to the jailers, "Welcome him!" Immediately, I was subjected to punches and kicks, beatings with batons and electric cables, and agents pressing on my face and head with their shoes. After two hours, I was thrown into a small, filthy cell. I could barely move and was stripped naked and resembled a lifeless body lying on the floor.

Difficult hours passed, hearing prisoners' screams. The captors spent the entire night torturing us one by one. I could not sleep: both the pain in my body and the fear I would be attacked again kept me awake.

In the morning, a guard opened the cell door, kicked me forcefully, pulled me up, tied my hands, and hit me repeatedly as he led me to the next room. Three other prisoners were there. They were physically drained and pale-faced and looked more like human remnants than humans.

Bits of food were brought to us, but our hands remained tied, so we had to crouch around the bowl and, taking turns, eat the food with our tongues like dogs. Blood still covered our faces and bodies.

Each prisoner was there for a different reason. My crime was that I had written an article about the situation in Syria that was critical of the state's actions against its citizens. For more than fifty years, Syrians have lived in fear under the oppression and tyranny of the Assad regime By March 2011, the Syrian people could no longer tolerate their dictator and took to the streets in an unarmed protest, asking for rights and freedoms.

The Syrian state responded with live bullets. There were many atrocious massacres, which international law classifies as "crimes against humanity." Half of Syria's citizens were displaced from their homes and country.

"Welcome to Canada."

The judge's words came after sixty difficult days of preparing documents to submit to the court so they could assess the asylum application I had made when I crossed the border in Niagara. A tear dropped as I received my right to protection. Everyone in the immigration courtroom was moved: my wife, the translator, and the lawyer. The impact of the judge's decision was reflected on her face and, looking at her through my tears, I felt an overwhelming sense of peace.

The first coffee I had after receiving my asylum and protection, in a café at Victoria and Adelaide in Toronto, refreshed my soul in a way that I still feel today. The rising steam of coffee reminded me of a time in Istanbul, when I stood on a high plateau and was taken aback by the beautiful view. I felt submerged in the clouds and fog, and a silence enveloped the place on that cold, early morning. It infused my restless soul with a serenity that lasted only for a moment, a serenity that eased the hurt and bitterness that had left harsh marks on my face and in my writings and speeches.

But I needed to continue my journey and began walking down into the valley, through the forest towards a small river. I felt a certain absence in this magical place, a feeling of confusion. It brought me back to the moment when the world was clouded through my eyes. As I walked down the remaining steps, I felt my heart stop, but it beat with patience, a patience that those who have experienced absence are aware of with certainty. I remembered the bitterness with every step I took.

In this city, there are a lot of stairs that you take up and down, to all destinations, every day, multiple times. A memory keeps me heavy, restricted. There were a few steps into the intelligence branch in Al-Khatib Street in Damascus. Four. As I was led down those steps by an officer who was pushing me inside the office, he uttered words that ring in my ears even today:

"A new guest ... teach him what freedom looks like!"

Four steps that I took calmly and in silence, and then my soul was transported to hell. Sealed rusty metal doors surrounded me on all sides, and behind each door was a prisoner exhausted from torture. In the corners, men stood ready to pounce on me like I was prey. I heard screams of those being tortured and saw traces of blood and smelled it. The warden commanded I put all I had on the table and strip myself of all my clothes.

And with the first club that hit my body, I thought I might not make it out of this place for a long time, if ever. But I was determined to stay strong rather than give up and be defeated inside.

The agent searched my bag, pulling out papers that included drafts of scattered poetic texts. He read some, then threw them on the table.

"You will write prettier poems than this here," he said. "The country is missing people like you, you traitors."

Then he proceeded to curse at me as he pushed me, naked, into a short corridor. He howled and described me as putrid gruel, his stinky breath and flying spit reminding me of Henri Charrière's insult of rotten meat in his novel *Papillon*.

He opened the cell door and pushed me inside so forcefully I fell to the floor. He stepped on my waist with his shoes, his teeth knocking miserably, making me lose any power to move. Then left and locked the door.

After some time, I was able to stand up again, with my clothes in my lap. I put them on slowly, leaning against a wall for support, then fell to the floor. I don't know how much time passed. My eyes circled in the darkness, exploring for any lines or letters on the wall, any scratching or other evidence left by the person who sat here before me. I searched for a crack in the door to see through, but to no avail. Fatigue entered my soul, my ribs were strained, my guts were shaken. I wet my lips with saliva as the cold trickled through me. I used my shoes as a pillow and lay for several minutes. Then the door opened, and the party of torture began. The beating didn't stop until I agreed to sign their interrogation report without knowing what was written in it.

Today, I fear re-experiencing what I went through. Can we explain the moments of pain, the hours of torture, the days, and years of arrest ... and can we forget about them, even if life has changed?

I cannot forget, even though eight years have passed. Despite my protection and safety in Canada, I've never been able to overcome the fear or expel my confrontation with death from my memory. I still fear writing about it, even though writing has stopped me from falling into the clutches of psychological imbalance. I was close to insanity and one second away from death in that cell, either from torture or asphyxiation.

I reached the centre of the valley and tried to cross the river through a rock passage lined with a layer of ice, which broke under my feet. I slipped and bounced back. A memory passed through my head of a punch I tried to avoid, only to receive a violent blow. I felt nothing but fog enveloping me like a dream, taking me far away among the stars. Finally, I crossed the river and sat on a nearby bench, covered in rainwater.

In the valley near Istanbul, I felt tight-chested as I recalled those memories from that terrible prison — the screams of the tortured, their naked bodies, torn and bloodied, the whispered words of another detainee: at night, you will hear scarier noises; you will hear the screams of the women, their pleas.

I looked around and there was no one but myself. Istanbul had opened its eyelids to my last day here. The next morning, I would be going to a riverbank far away, on another continent beyond the Atlantic. I would leave the magic of this city, the warmth it brings to strangers, and the safety that I missed. The city welcomed me as a passing stranger but did not recognize me as a refugee survivor of prison and death. Istanbul, with spaces of limited freedom, and the fear and torture that lived within us. Her many high steps that tired my heart going up and burned my soul going down, as if I were entering the cell once again.

I want to leave everything behind me: the torture, the years in prison and absence from family and children, the smell of dusty roads, the fear and panic that have haunted me for many years to the point where I cannot sleep peacefully, and I cannot walk in neighbourhoods without being overwhelmed by the feeling that someone is watching me.

I want to learn how one forgets all that torture and worry for a second … just one second! Writing has always liberated me from fear and saved me from depression and psychological weakness, but to this day, eight years since my last arrest, I still struggle to write about the horrendous and monstrous torture I endured, let alone what other victims experienced, because their torture was often more gruesome than mine. I had watched them die from torture and deliberate medical neglect.

But I must write for the sake of the victims: those who are absent, and those still under Syrian arrest. For their sake, and for others tasting bitterness, torture, and deprivation.

The Road to Canada

The survivor of prison, of the Syrian regime and its allies in the war against people demanding freedom and democracy, becomes homeless, a refugee, he must search for a place to stay. That is the case for twelve million Syrians who have been forced out of their homes; many of those homes have been destroyed.

Like other Syrian writers and journalists, I was subjected to threats of arrest and death by the Syrian regime, the Al-Nusra Front, and isis, who wrote my name on their blacklist with seventy other Syrian writers and journalists. I tried to find an escape, which included an attempt across the sea towards the unknown.

In Riyadh, Saudi Arabia, Canada refused to give me a visitor visa, even though my wife had permanent residency in Canada. But I couldn't stay in a country that did not respect human rights like Saudi Arabia, Turkey,

Lebanon, Iraq, or Libya. However, luck was my ally, and after a long interview with the American consulate in Riyadh, I was finally granted a visitor visa to the United States. I began preparing to leave the Middle East for New York.

Just hours after receiving the visa, a respected doctor informed me that an American visa does not guarantee entry to the United States, and he listed examples, even his own. Then a Syrian reporter in Istanbul told me that they had returned him from the Washington airport, despite having a visa and making repeated visits to the U.S. in the past two years. The stories caused me a hell of worry.

I was certain that I could not board my flight, but I had no choice but to try. I left Riyadh and spent a week in Istanbul in the company of my son. I had spent little time with him over the years due to my imprisonment and homelessness. He had become a young man on the verge of a new life after being displaced from one country to the other because of wars caused by tyrannical regimes. He'd gone from Libya to Syria and finally, Turkey.

My son was by my side in the Istanbul airport as I took faint steps in the lineup for a U.S. security check and to get my boarding pass. I was talking to him, pretending not to be drowning in worry. But he could see through me, and knowing I was anxious, he grabbed my fingers and started joking about things. I don't remember what he said, or perhaps I never heard his words, as I was listening to my fear as it moved inside me. Heavy seconds passed before the American security agent returned my passport and allowed me to pass.

The plane felt crowded and suffocating. I was constantly thinking of what awaited me at John F. Kennedy Airport. When we arrived, I exited the plane slowly, dragging my feet towards an uncertain future. I found myself in front of a smiling officer who looked into my eyes as he held my passport and welcomed me like an old friend. Then he asked if I needed help as he returned my passport with a fresh entry stamp. His kindness confused me — having only experienced border crossings in oppressive countries, I was used to mistreatment to the point of humiliation. I held my only bag and stood in the hallway to recover from my astonishment.

But a person interrupted my trance before I could catch my breath, pointing to the door:

"This way, sir."

As I moved, I saw the smiling face of my friend and host.

I had planned to spend a week in one of the most important cities in the world. But on the road to my host's home from the airport, we passed the UN headquarters, Times Square, and the famous Hudson River, and yet instead of enjoying the sights, I was anxious and tense, and no longer thirsty to explore a city as big as New York.

The next morning, I decided to cut my New York stay short and head to Canada earlier than planned. My friend said the road north would not be safe as there was a snowstorm hitting the area of western New York and southern Ontario where the border crossing was. But I held to my desire to leave. Something was driving me: I wanted escape. Though I was no longer under threat of the Syrian regime, I still felt the need to escape the fear, worries, and fatigue and reach my final destination.

My state of mind was similar to when I signed the interrogation report at the intelligence branch, without caring about the charges against me after fifty continuous hours of cruel and horrific torture. I wanted to rest, and I wanted the situation to end, regardless of the consequences.

My friend offered to drive me to the Canadian border. I will never forget his support and hospitality.

Eagerly, we embarked on an adventure towards the border crossing in Buffalo. The weather reports were accurate, and we encountered a severe snowstorm. It was the first snowstorm I'd experienced in almost fifty-five years of living. We needed to stop for the night.

We continued our journey the next morning, and that began the adventure of entering Canada without a visa. When we reached the highest point of the Peace Bridge, I looked down at the Niagara River. My friend whispered, smiling:

"We just left the United States: we are in neutral territory. Ahead is the gate to Canada."

I did not know peace till that day. A tear escaped my right eye and fell to my cheek as I continued staring at the river.

Though I was looking at the Niagara River, I saw the Euphrates: the evening stories on its banks, the torment of years at the hands of a dictator and ISIS ... memories soaked in torture, prisons, death, and displacement. Yet they were all in the past.

"He does not have a visa; he wishes to apply for refuge," said my friend at the Canadian gates in response to the officer's short questions. The officer asked us to go to the main office in the opposite building.

We entered the immigration office; I gave my ID and passport, then sat waiting my turn to be seen.

No one arrested me for not having an entry visa, I was not handcuffed by police, and they did not curse at me or hit me. Most people would say that is normal in a country where everything is governed by laws. But such is not the case in my country, where, if you want to travel, you must obtain prior approval. It is not easy to get a passport, and when you try to leave you might be arrested for something as simple as a name similarity or the intelligence officer not liking your appearance.

In my country, if you go back to your homeland, you might not be allowed to leave the airport except to go to prison, for something as simple as having had coffee with a person whose political views do not align with the government. In the best-case scenario, you will be forced to pay bribes to the customs officer or immigration police and then humiliated and insulted as you complete the entry procedure.

The immigration office in Niagara was not satisfied with a picture of my wife's permanent residency card and insisted that she be present, but she was three hours away in Toronto.

In the waiting area, we were hosted by an NGO. They offered us food and drinks, gathered all our personal information in order to communicate later, and then withdrew from the scene so the police could take their turn. They took me to a separate room and searched my luggage thoroughly. I don't blame them for doing so: I was coming from one of the most terrorist-filled countries in the world, where the Islamic government had made their state in my city, Raqqa. The paradox is that Assad's regime is not looked on as a government that supports and produces terror, when in reality it is not much different from ISIS and Al-Qaida. Canada and the United States are well aware of that.

The investigator was not concerned that the person in front of him was a writer and a journalist; he thought I could be a fighter or a member in a terrorist organization!

The translator arrived and finally, my wife, but she had to stay outside. We were not allowed to meet, even though others at the immigration office were allowed to see their family members. I felt a sense of discrimination that I traced to being Middle Eastern.

The police started investigating me. It was a long, bitter, and tiring process. I answered questions with great patience, to the point where I began to feel oppressed and thought that I must end this torment, cut the investigation short, cancel my asylum request, and get out; whatever happens, happens. The translator was urging me to be patient as I returned to the hospitality room to rest for a few minutes, my eyes red and full of tears, only to be comforted by the immigration employees, who offered me water, coffee, and apples.

The officer did not know that I was remembering the bitter investigations of the past, where I was tortured in intelligence branches, airports, basements, and jail cells. I was immersed in the darkness of oppression and torture that I still have not recovered from to this day.

After eight exhausting hours, I received documentation to enter and was ordered to appear in court in two months' time. With that, the officer finally flashed a brief smile as she helped me drag my luggage outside the building where I fell into my wife's arms and breathed fresh air. Then, we took the road to Toronto.

Canada: The Challenges

Eight years have passed since my arrival in Canada. I received temporary residency then citizenship, and I now feel safe and at peace, and I practise all my rights and freedoms without prejudice or violation from anybody. But I faced challenges along the way.

I was not able to reunite with my children for seven years. The selective "humanitarian" view of Canada's immigration policy deprived me of that. Despite promises made by two ministries — Global Affairs and Immigration — to solve this problem, for many writers and journalists the promises remain empty words.

No government or non-government organization contacted me to offer psychological support as a new immigrant who had been imprisoned and tortured — a victim needing treatment. I did not receive financial support. I hoped to receive welfare, but my wife supported and covered all our expenses and care until I started working.

In Canada, to work in your specialization, you must have the "Canadian perspective." For someone like me, it is impossible to work in journalism; you have to work in the available professional positions in the public service and factories, whether you are a writer, journalist, doctor, or engineer. The Canadian policy of integrating immigrants into the workforce is unfair and unjust. My poor English language skills were a barrier to my ability to build networks, to receive community support, including the right job. But this did not stop me from integrating into the community and workforce. I was able to create multiple cultural activities and I participated in many cultural events. As a result, I am proud to have received an award for empowering communities and for my dedication to the arts.

Nevertheless, I work full time as a night-shift employee at the Magna car parts factory north of Toronto. My job takes a lot of physical strength and drains my energy. After eight hours of work, I need another eight hours of sleep and relaxation. As I write these pages, I find I've lost eight kilos because of work stress! And I find no time to read or write most days.

With no opportunities to publish in Canadian newspapers or other online sites, it's like being deprived of life, as writing is the oxygen that I breathe and the way I see the world. It is like being arrested deprived me of writing, and from that point I was no longer allowed to publish a poem or an article.

Today, I work as a loader in the factory, supplying the lines with production materials and supplies. I think about the shapes of coins, how they turn into words in a poem. I write texts in my mind and then they are lost. When I throw out the trash every morning at half-past five, I hear the sounds of Carl Orff's *Carmina Burana*, which I merge with recurring memories from my life: prison, writing, and travelling. Suddenly, the supervisor's voice comes to me: "Hey ... Abdul ... Wake up!"

I dream of having the time or another job that would allow me the opportunity to write a new poem, a new book. For now, the poet is the loader.

Mahdi Saremifar
(Iran)

MAHDI SAREMIFAR is an Iranian journalist. He was a science correspondent for *Hamshahri*, one of the most read newspapers in Iran, and editor-in-chief of an Iranian popular science magazine. He was forced to leave Iran when the science he was reporting conflicted with the doctrines of the Supreme Leader.

In Defence of Science and Rationality

I COME FROM Iran, a land in the Middle East, an ancient country at the crossroads of history. In the easternmost part of the Fertile Crescent, the Iranian Plateau has been the host of ancient civilizations for millennia. Twenty-five centuries ago, Cyrus the Great liberated the Jewish captives of Nebuchadnezzar and established a united kingdom in this land — Iran.

Iranians were among Mesopotamia's flag-bearers of human culture for half a millennium in the medieval era. In particular, they have played an essential role in the intellectual richness of Islamic civilization and its development in the West.

Our knowledge about Iran is incomplete unless we look at the element of religion. For nearly four hundred years, the 'Shiite' religion, one of the sub-branches of mainstream Islam, had established a strong connection with the sovereignty and monarchy in Iran.

The country's rapid growth after the oil crisis of the early 1970s and the attempt to grant broad social and economic freedoms, especially for women and religious and sexual minorities, at the end of the decade had a strange and unbelievable result: the 1979 Iranian Revolution. The result was the cleric regime of the Islamic Republic of Iran.

For more than forty years, our country has been ruled by the 'Guardianship of the Islamic Jurist' regime (*Velâyat-e Faqih*), a totalitarian tyranny. It is based on an interpretation of a verse of the Qur'an, putting all matters of governance under the supervision of a Shiite jurist with special conditions: the Supreme Leader (*Vali Faqih*).

Iran has been one of the darkest places in the world in terms of human rights during these four decades. Among the Ayatollah's records are: hundreds of executions per year, long prison terms for those protesting the economic situation, anti-women and anti-2SLGBTQ+ rights laws, imprisonment or execution of people of the Baha'i faith, and lack of freedom for people to choose the type of clothing they wear — especially women, for whom the hijab is compulsory.

Enmity with poets, writers, and journalists has been regular from day one in this regime. Hundreds of writers and journalists have been imprisoned and executed for their intellectual works and writing under the pretext of "Acting Against National Security" since the 1980s.

Saeedi Sirjani, a poet and member of the Iranian Writers' Association (PEN Iran), was executed forty years ago. Baktash Abtin, secretary of the Iranian Writers' Association, died in January 2022 due to a lack of access to medical facilities in prison during the pandemic. Asghar Amirani, an editor-in-chief, was executed in 1980. Zahra Kazemi, an Iranian Canadian journalist and photographer, was killed in the dreaded Evin prison two decades ago. Sattar Beheshti, a blogger, was killed when he was punched and kicked in a police detention centre. Ruhollah Zam, a journalist, was executed in December 2020. These are just a few of the names of well-known Iranian journalists and writers who have been killed by this brutal regime.

In addition, 'The Chain Murders of Iran' should be added to this list: this systematic murder of writers and intellectuals was exposed in 1998, revealing that the murders were carried out by top security officials close to the Supreme Leader. In those days, when the enthusiasm for reformist activities against extremist Islamists had become the driving force of Iranian society, my story as a journalist began.

From Newsstand to Editorial Board

In the 1990s, when I was still a teenager going to high school, there was a biweekly magazine I loved very much: *Danestaniha*. I waited two weeks for each issue to appear on the newsstand and eagerly bought it. The internet was not yet popularized in Iran at the time, and satellite TV was banned (a ban that has continued). Thus, *Danestaniha* (which means 'Knowledge' in English) was my only window to the outside world.

This magazine significantly shaped my mentality and interest as a journalist in science and technology. The magazine encouraged me to enter the STEM (Science, Technology, Engineering, and Mathematics) world. Thus, in the same days that were dubbed the 'Press Spring' in Iran, I joined the university to study Physics. The path that started from there, ten years later took me to the position of editor-in-chief of *Danestaniha* magazine, the way of science and rationality.

I will never forget the day I wrote my first report for a national newspaper. I was writing stories about scientific discoveries and innovations for our university's internal newspaper. The Space Shuttle *Columbia* disaster was a fatal incident, killing all its astronauts. The science editor of a high-circulation newspaper, who had read a short article I had written about the shuttle tragedy, became interested, and she allowed me to publish a more complete article about that incident for their newspaper. Less than a year later, I edited a daily page to cover scientific news in the newspaper *Hamshahri*, the most globally circulated Persian-language newspaper.

The Extent of Censorship, from the Weather Situation to the Number of Scientific Papers

The first thing that might have come to your mind was probably the question of what science and technology journalism has to do with politics and why it should be censored. If this conjecture is true, you must have never experienced living under a totalitarian dictatorship!

Since 2005, the Supreme Leader has been falsely claiming the development of science and technology are priorities. He promised the country would become the first economic and scientific power in the Middle East in an ambitious, twenty-year plan. This was the beginning of the propaganda about science. Since then, state and military officials have been trying to show that they are continuing to move closer to their original goals from the first year.

One of the focal points of the then Minister of Science, Research, and Technology was research and development in Nanotechnology. Naturally, I covered these issues daily in the newspaper (and sometimes on the national radio). At the time, I concluded that these indicators were not accurate. The quality of scientific papers is more important. My reports and interviews met with a negative reaction from the government.

I was invited to the presidential Special Staff for Nanotechnology Development office for a "friendly" conversation. But contrary to expectations, my host was not a scholar or a scientific official. He was, instead, an officer from the security department of the organization.

He led me to a room in the security department, and I was interrogated there for about four hours. The interrogator first verbally accused me of counter-revolution under the influence of the enemy's propaganda. But then the level of verbal violence began to steadily decline, and the interrogator took on a kind tone.

On another day, I saw my interrogator on the street by chance. I found out that, in addition to being a security officer of the Special Staff for Nanotechnology Development, he is also one of the censorship agents in the Ministry of Culture.

The Ministry of Culture of the Islamic Republic supervises all content developed in the country. Anyone who wants to write a book (fiction or non-fiction), produce a movie, create music, develop software and/or a video game, run a website, or even have a popular channel on a social network (like Instagram or Telegram) has to get permission twice from the ministry: once at the start of the process (for example, filming) and once prior to publishing.

You may remember the Ministry of Truth in George Orwell's novel *1984*. The day I saw my interrogator, he held a copy of the original Persian translation of Khaled Hosseini's novel *The Kite Runner*. He said that the ministry had given it to him to read and censor before it could be granted a publishing permit.

One thing I will never forget was the harsh winter of 2008. That year, President Ahmadinejad, who was close to the hardliners and the favourite of the Supreme Leader, suspended the Daylight Saving Act in Iran. Ironically, a severe and unusual cold prevailed in the country when winter came. People could not access the national gas network because of decreased pressure. The energy balance in the country was upset. Energy did not reach some parts of the country; unfortunately, some died due to the cold and lack of resources.

At the same time, a confidential circular reached our daily newspaper, *Hamshahri*, as well as other media. Temperatures in some parts were below -10 degrees Celsius and storms and cold swept across much of the country. But according to this confidential letter, we had to show the temperature as zero degrees Celsius and the situation as sunny.

Self-censorship: A Tool for the Repression of Journalists

In the early days of my career, I realized that the most important means of controlling and suppressing journalists were not governmental and intelligence institutions outside the newspaper. Rather, the censorship process began inside the editorial office. In most editorial boards, the editors-in-chief have assistants in charge of "monitoring" (censoring). They read your text in steps before publishing and marked the parts they did not find appropriate. Therefore, if Iranian journalists wanted to publish their reports, they were obliged to do everything that these censorship agents had specified. This practice continues today.

My experience is tied to one of many of the greatest genocides in human history. I was the editor of the "Science and the World" section for a popular youth magazine when President Ahmadinejad denied the Holocaust in a speech. So, at the editorial board meeting that week we decided to write about the Holocaust, and there was no further talk.

Over a week, I did extensive research on the Third Reich genocide against the Jewish people: the quotations from Adolf Hitler in *Mein Kampf*, the painful images of Dachau and Auschwitz, quotations of victims who had been the witness of genocide, and the evidence that the Allies gathered from those camps, and so on. The pre-release version of the report reached the editor-in-chief of the magazine.

That day, the editor put aside all those facts and figures on his desk and told me, "You were wrong! You should have written something that would support the president's claim!"

I stood up. "This is a big lie. Why should we not write against this lie? He is the president, not the Supreme Leader who represents *Allah*," I answered him.

But the editor told me, "This is the beloved president of the Supreme Leader! If we publish this report, the magazine will be shut down." This was true; this magazine usually rejected the facts that are as bright as day without any worries. I declined to write the factually incorrect piece, and the favourable report of the Ministry of Truth was written by someone else.

Self-censorship is encouraged in all media. One of my specialties in journalism is nuclear technologies. I have been covering this issue in the media since the first days when the case of the Islamic Republic's nuclear activities was raised in the UN Security Council. One of my problems with the editors at the time was that they (or the system) tended not to tell the Iranian public about the dual nature of the technology.

In a report published in the same journal, I described the Possible Military Dimension (PMD) of nuclear programs. But I was rejecting the magazine editor's self-censorship requests. Our dispute escalated, and eventually, the report was not published. A few days later, when I went to the magazine's office, one of the editors told me that the editor-in-chief wanted me to stop coming to the magazine!

The printing press is the last step in censoring and preventing the spread of journalists' voices. Unfortunately, the foundation of the printed media in Iran is fragile, and many do not have a dedicated printing press. The Ministry of Culture also has censorship agents in the printing presses.

In the days following the 2009 elections, I worked for a daily newspaper belonging to one of the protest leaders. The printing press repeatedly distorted our reports about fraud in announcing the election results. Hence, part of the newspaper page was blank when printed! This was not uncommon. Printing presses then and now regularly distort the ink and the film (or even pdf files) submitted by the editorial offices. In those days, the government filtered many influential websites and banned communication channels. They even cut off the cellphone messages system.

Livelihood, Subsistence, and Death Threats

Being fired, feeling pressured to self-censor, and suffering interrogation in the Ministry of Intelligence are not the only ways the voices of journalists and writers are stifled by the Islamic Republic. These are just the beginning and are used mainly against *junior* journalists. If they do not cooperate, the regime of the Islamic Republic will use other tools: put journalists' lives and livelihoods at risk, cause them to lose their jobs, shut down the media, imprison the journalist, and even impose the death penalty.

In 2010, a few months had passed since the beginning of the nation-wide protests of the Iranian people. Widespread repression and censorship prevailed in Iran. The government had arrested many citizens and even killed several on the street. Political activists and journalists were also in prison. In addition, the regime broadcast televised confessions every few days, similar to what was done in the Soviet Union.

I worked in Tehran for a magazine owned by one of the protest leaders. One day, my colleague called me and showed me something interesting. He opened the second page of the magazine, which displayed the list of the editorial team: a column of eleven names and titles. The names appearing on the first to the eighth rows had been arrested, imprisoned, or temporarily released on bail. The names on rows ten and eleven were my friend and me, and in row nine was the name of another of my colleagues. "It seems that the intelligence and security system of the Islamic Republic has put this list in front of it and is ordering us to court," my friend said as a joke.

We decided to leave the city temporarily. We escaped to the north of Iran that night. When my friend got into my car, the first thing he said was very shocking: the wife of our colleague (on row nine of the editorial list) had called and said that he had not come home yet and that his cellphone was off.

We were worried. Our colleague was not heard from for several days until he called home and said he had been arrested and was currently in prison. We were relieved that he was at least alive and well, and we laughed that our prediction had been correct. We stayed away in a small village in northern Iran in hopes of changing the situation. The government eventually shut down the magazine.

Creating problems for the livelihood of journalists is a common way to discourage them from pursuing media activities. Usually, many *junior* journalists work in Iranian newspapers and news agencies, and you are unlikely to see people with a long history on an editorial board.

The reason is that the Islamic Republic is encouraging its loyal journalists to take on positions as public relations managers of governmental companies and institutes. These journalists have agreed to work with the anti-freedom of expression apparatus and censorship system.

If you oppose this system, unemployment, imprisonment, exile, and immigration await you. Hence, many senior Iranian journalists are either outside Iran or have left journalism to support themselves and their families in other jobs.

I was in at least nine editorial offices, all of which were closed by the Islamic Republic. For many experienced people, this number may reach twenty. My journalistic skills are noteworthy. Despite this, in the last ten years, I have been unemployed for almost half of that time. Every time we tried to start a new media outlet (especially a printed one), the government shut it down.

One of the best efforts in modern journalism in Iran after the 2009 protests was the daily newspaper *Mardom Emrooz*. The project started with accurate planning, and I witnessed the launch of one of Iran's highest-quality press editorial boards in the last twenty years. Unfortunately, it was closed just three weeks after the launch out of sympathy for the *Charlie Hebdo* cartoonists and journalists.

Such shocks, including dismissals and shutting down of the media, have caused a great deal of disaster for journalists' subsistence. But physical elimination is the Islamic Republic's final tool to suppress journalists and writers.

Sometimes the judiciary kills writers with official means, from the execution of various writers in the 1980s through to the execution of journalist Ruhollah Zam in 2020. Sometimes the security system eliminates writers and journalists by highly suspicious means, such as the linked "chain murders" of Iranian writers. The story of the Iranian Writers' Association's (PEN Iran) trip to Armenia was a strange instance.

In the summer of 1996, a group of Iranian writers, poets, and journalists travelled by bus to Armenia at the invitation of the Writers' Association of Armenia. These Iranian writers were unaware that the security forces of the Islamic Republic had decided to get rid of them by shooting at the bus carrying them to the event. But the vigilance of the bus passengers prevented this attack.

For me, too, the threat of murder has occurred in unofficial ways. Let's skip the ordinary and insignificant threats on social networks. I receive one of these almost every month. Especially now that I'm in Canada, I can share my ideas with the public without censorship. Yet the threat of being murdered persists. Otherwise, cyberbullying on social networks such as Twitter and Instagram is routine.

My story in this regard is tied to the crimes of the oppressive regime of Bashar al-Assad. When Assad faced the revolution of the Syrian people, he confronted the Syrian citizens with the most brutal means possible. The Islamic Revolutionary Guard Corps (IRGC), which had been able to suppress the protests of the Iranian people in 2009, aided Assad's regime. The IRGC (Quds Force) terrorist unit commander prepared a large army from Iran, Iraq, Afghanistan, and Pakistan. This force has been involved in all of the crimes of Bashar al-Assad in the last ten years.

My writings against complicity in this crime culminated in 2014. At that time, a series of government propaganda pieces suddenly began in defence of the commander of the Quds Force, the Iranian perpetrator of the Syrian crimes. In the government propaganda, Qasem Soleimani was portrayed as a brave commander who fought for his homeland in Syria. When I first posted these tragedies on Facebook, I received daily warnings.

At that time, I was the editor of the weekend supplement of the daily newspaper *Hamshahri*. In a detailed Facebook post, I explained why complicity in Bashar al-Assad's crimes was the most significant blow to Iran's national interests. The next day, my supervisor suddenly sent a message that the newspaper manager had asked me not to come to the office tomorrow. I had been fired, but the story did not end there. I received the most serious death threat that day. The source of the threat was not an unknown person: he was my colleague.

Since that day, I have not failed to cover the events in Syria and the crimes of the Assad regime and the Quds Force. Unfortunately, the Iranian people are subjected to extremely vigorous government propaganda, which claims that these crimes on Syrian soil are, in fact, to defend the homeland. It is a big lie, and these military activities of the IRGC in Iraq, Syria, Lebanon, Yemen, Bahrain, Afghanistan, and so on, have only one goal: to spread Shiite orthodoxy. The Supreme Leader has spoken on this issue many times.

Absolute Repression in Science and Technology Journalism

Yes, this absolute repression is extraordinary, especially in the areas where the Supreme Leader of the Islamic Republic speaks publicly and explicitly. If the Ayatollah speaks about science and technology, even if what he claims is wrong or pseudo-science, the media is required to write about it and confirm it. No comments against his views or criticisms of his opinions are allowed in any official media.

The most important example in this regard is the issue of COVID-19 vaccines. When vaccines entered the phase of public approval and the prospect of the world emerging from a pandemic, the Ayatollah banned the import of any vaccines from the United States and Britain in a televised public speech. He claimed that the enemy had designed these to be tested on the Iranian people.

This order, and his pseudo-scientific explanations, led to the banning of the Pfizer, Moderna, and AstraZeneca vaccines in Iran. The resulting delay in nationwide vaccination resulted in the deaths of at least 100,000 more Iranian citizens.

I know almost all the major Iranian science desk editors. They are literate and have access to the resources needed to critique the pseudo-scientific issues raised in the Supreme Leader's speech banning coronavirus vaccines. Absolutely none of them was able to publish an article or report criticizing this speaker in Iranian publications.

At the beginning of the coronavirus epidemic, the Islamic Revolutionary Guard Corps unveiled a device called Musta'an-110. They claimed that the device could detect the coronavirus from a distance of one hundred metres using radio waves. This claim goes against the laws of nature. But this device was hailed in the official Iranian media as an outstanding scientific achievement and received national coverage. The only print media outlet that reported the inaccuracy of the case was the *Danstaniha* magazine. I was the editor-in-chief; it was my last year as editor-in-chief before I immigrated to Canada.

In recent years, the nuclear program of the Islamic Republic of Iran in uranium enrichment has attracted the attention of world powers, who have imposed sanctions on Iran for these activities. Policymakers in the Islamic Republic, especially the Supreme Leader, claim that Iran's nuclear activities have no military application and are purely peaceful. However, no official media in Iran can examine these claims from a technical point of view and publish the results.

This is precisely the case with the missile program too. In recent years, the Islamic Republic has launched several satellites under the auspices of military institutions such as the Ministry of Defence and the Islamic Revolutionary Guard Corps (IRGC). The propaganda of the Islamic Republic in the public sphere is that this scientific research has brought Iran to the cutting edge of technology. But media coverage of these achievements is not like that of other scientific achievements.

Any newspaper or website hosted on servers inside Iran must publish only the official press release announcements. No media outlet can post a review of these activities. However, the hardware and the development path of these projects align with the North Korean government's ability to achieve intercontinental ballistic missiles capable of carrying nuclear warheads.

The Supreme Leader of the Islamic Republic and the commanders of the IRGC feel free to comment on almost any scientific subject, even though the Ayatollah only reached the eighth year of education. They claim to have expertise on subjects such as increasing the birth rate, the size of an edible chicken, and limits of quantum science.

In such circumstances, science and technology journalism is one of the few fields that cannot survive in Iran and address the country's fundamental issues as long as the government threatens it with interrogation, imprison-ment, and death.

But the defence of science and rationality is not exhaustive. Fortu-nately, the possibilities of cyberspace have come to the aid of the Iranian people. Many Iranian journalists, writers, and intellectuals — in exile or forced out of Iran — pursue news activities and continue to enlighten the Iranian people. However, we sometimes hear that the regime plans to assassinate or kidnap opposition journalists in New York or set traps to execute a writer in Paris.

This battle continues for science and rationality …

Ava Homa
(Kurdish)

AVA HOMA is an award-winning Kurdish-Canadian writer and activist. Her debut novel, *Daughters of Smoke and Fire* (HarperCollins), won the 2020 Silver Nautilus Award for fiction and was a finalist for the 2022 William Saroyan International Writing Prize. Her book of short stories *Echoes from the Other Land* was nominated for the 2011 Frank O'Connor Short Story Prize. Homa's articles have appeared in *The Globe and Mail*, BBC, *Toronto Star*, *Literary Hub*, and *Literary Review of Canada*, among many others. Ava holds a master's degree in creative writing from the University of Windsor. The chapter following this introduction is from her bestselling book, *Daughters of Smoke and Fire*, and is reprinted with the permission of the publisher.

INTRODUCTION
Making Space for Each Other's Stories

Having lived approximately half of my forty years of life in Kurdistan and the rest in North America, I've caught glimpses of the East and the West, which I consider the two sides of the collective human brain. That's why despite the atrocities I've witnessed, I am grateful for the exposure and the expansion that ensued. From being persecuted in Iran for my writing and activism, to being uprooted and overlooked in Canada, to eventually receiving critical acclaim in outlets such as *The Globe and Mail* and the *Toronto Star* for my debut novel *Daughters of Smoke and Fire* (Harper-Collins, 2020), my personal odyssey has taught me the power of stories to connect us.

Coming of age as a Kurdish girl in Iran, I learned early on that my being alive was an act of subversion. I belong to a people who have been subject to repeated genocides. Ever since the Allies redrew the map of the Middle East after World War I, we have been under attack by four atrocious states that have perceived us as threats to be annihilated, never as humans. From the 1937–1938 Dersim massacre at the hands of the Turkish government, Saddam Hussein's 1986–1988 Anfal genocide in Iraq, the attacks and ongoing executions in Iran, to the massacre in Syria, Kurds are a nation that has been denied a state of its own and, consequently, we have been denied the right to exist and live in peace.

I was raised with hushed stories of massacres and how we survived them. How state soldiers, even volunteer militia, came to our cities and villages to kill us, to more than kill us. They gassed us, torched our villages, raped our women, shot fathers before the wide eyes of their children … and more, much more.

In spite of — or perhaps because of — all of that, Kurds became masters of rising from the ashes. Our statelessness killed us but also taught us to resurrect. It's no wonder that our most common mantra has become *Barxodan Jiana*: Resistance is life.

Resistance Is Life

Kurds, like many indigenous nations around the globe, have experienced enormous suffering and intergenerational trauma, but that's not the whole story. We deal with state-run violence and internal tyranny and yet the ocean of grief that my people have carried has offered them an exemplary depth of soul. They love and are loved by their land. They're connected to their rivers and mountains, and to their multi-religion communities. They'll offer you, any guest, the best portion of their limited food without hesitation. They look out for strangers the way they look out for their own. To an unkind world ravished by greed, violence, and short-sightedness, Kurds can present compassion and resilience.

The complex realities of my ancestry, coupled with my sensitivities, made me a writer and activist at a young age, had me take on more than my share of suffering, and eventually put my life in danger. I interviewed, wrote about, and felt accountable to political prisoners languishing under torture and on death rows in the nefarious Iranian prisons, to families whose loved ones were executed for fighting for justice, and to those escaping war and destruction only to be stuck in refugee camps or lose their lives while running away. Their stories urged me to turn pain into poetry, grief into strength, oppression into resilience.

Although I remain too powerless to make structural changes, I learned along the way that listening and bearing witness to other people's stories healed me and healed them. Making space for others expanded my consciousness, showed me how unimportant I was, and that realization liberated me from crippling self-pity, despair, and fear.

Searching for safety, I applied to, gained admission, and won a scholarship to study for my master's degree in English and creative writing at the University of Windsor in Ontario. Canada, my beloved, imperfect, adopted homeland, let me experience safety but more importantly handed me a priceless perspective. Canada's diversity — minimally reflected in its literature — liberated me from my limited views.

At first, I was mainly exposed to the stories of the settlers. Then I dug and learned about the residential schools, the Japanese internment camps, the struggles of newcomers like me, and the overall realities of all the marginalized groups. The exposure made me realize that the oppressor and the oppressed lived everywhere, including within me. There was nowhere on Earth I could go to find absolute justice.

Exiled, stateless, and uprooted as I was, suddenly, I wasn't alone anymore. When I opened my heart to the multitude of stories, I understood myself better, but beyond that, I understood what I had only known only theoretically: the interconnectedness, the oneness.

This is not to disregard my negative experiences in Canada. Early on, I learned that although I wasn't silenced here, I wasn't heard either. I noticed the hierarchy of voices, opinions, and stories. Not only was I "a person of colour" despite my fair skin, but I was also almost non-existent in the POC category where the First Nations, the Jews, Blacks, Asians, and others had to fight hard to be heard.

I watched in distress as politicians and commentators discussed "immigration policy," as if the spectrum of refugees and migrants was a single canvas they could paint with their apprehension or compassion. We're not seen as diverse humans whose history and destiny were shaped by the whim and the interim interests of the men in power. I was appalled by the downright racist job market, disheartened by the discriminatory publishing world, and at one point fully disillusioned.

Yet, I had a responsibility, an untold story to write. For me, being a Kurdish-Canadian writer-in-exile has been about rebirth and resistance. The precarious life of Kurds has travelled through history and will continue to do so. If I do what I know how to do, at the very least, I can show that even in the age of nation-states, stateless Kurds matter, and we are as complicated, important, imperfect, funny, and fascinating as any other group of humans. Perhaps if we are reminded of our humanity — of Kurds, of everyone — we can create global policies that reflect that.

So, for ten years, I put blood and sweat into crafting a novel I wrote in my third language. In *Daughters of Smoke and Fire* — which won America's Nautilus Book Award for fiction and was a finalist for the William Saroyan International Writing Prize — my protagonist, Leila, is an aspiring filmmaker searching for her abducted activist brother. She's crushed under the cruelties and injustices, overwhelmed by cultural and social pressures.

There's too much to bear, let alone process. Then she comes face to face with her mortality. A gun is held to her head.

Facing death, a curtain drops before Leila's eyes; the lies and illusions, promoted by dark forces like warlords, some politicians, and corporations disappear. Leila sees her trajectory as part of the collective chaos and pain. In that moment of clarity, she sees beyond her own pain, she sees the gas chambers, the internment camps, the plantations. Suffering is no longer an indication of her unworthiness, but part of the human condition.

For me, diverse stories are an invitation to expand our consciousness, to grow as individuals *and* as members of a global society. What is happening in our world today — the awe of technology, the lives lost and divided between the oceans, pandemics that mock our borders — are important wake-up calls trying to liberate us from the illusion of separation. I don't mean to undermine our valuable differences since we each bring unique experiences to this world. Rather, I'm reflecting on our precious connection as the human species with short, truly fragile lives.

My writing is an invitation to bear witness to the realities of an unheard people. Bearing witness to the suffering of others is not easy, nor is it taught anywhere. It requires courage and space-making and that needs willingness and persistence. But once suffering is understood for what it is, then comes the ability to see the light beyond it. We have a higher tolerance for suffering than we think. We all enter this world crying.

Looking away won't diminish the pain and instead only reinforces it. So, let's take a deep breath and make space for each other. The pain that temporarily rises vaccinates us and is the first step in healing ourselves and others.

The weight of human suffering, of injustice and oppression, is on our backs, on everyone. To what extent one is aware of this collective pressure differs from individual to individual. Yet, we intuitively know that our personal healing is intertwined with our collective healing and the first step is listening and bearing witness.

We can't let ourselves be swallowed into the hollowness of bad news, by the modern black hole of mass media that passes off indifference and apathy as professionalism and bombards our psyches by reporting one disaster after the other. They leave us to process all that on our own, and eventually we look away, afraid and overwhelmed. Media, unlike literature, mainly focuses on sorrow, rarely strength, showing us the destruction, but little of the rebuilding.

An expanded consciousness has a larger tolerance for suffering in and around us. The inner peace it brings will help us treat our neighbours differently or let the accented foreigner who has escaped catastrophes breathe in this gorgeous, generous land. We will understand — not only in our heads but in our bodies — that "others" are not a burden and a threat as populists need us to believe. They're a treasure of experience and once they're heard and valued — not merely "tolerated" — our collective energies integrate and build on each other. We will fully understand that this beautiful, gracious, resilient planet has enough for all of us if we treat it right. At this very moment, there's enough wealth in this world that no one should stay hungry and cold and no more of our environment should be destroyed.

As more of us practise expansion on a regular basis, shift internally, and grow compassionate, the ocean of human suffering will shrink to a river; we will all find balance. Because if I make space for your story and you make space for mine, our world will become more spacious one person at a time.

Excerpt from
Daughters of Smoke and Fire

WHEN HIS GRANDPA drew a yogurt moustache above Alan's lips, the boy dissolved into giggles. Picturing himself with real whiskers thrilled Alan, who thought that facial hair might make up for being shorter than the other boys in his class.

"Your laughter woke me up, you cheeky monkey!" Uncle Soran, youngest of the six uncles and the only one awake, tousled Alan's hair as he came onto the patio that opened to the yard. They sat around a nylon cloth spread atop a crimson handmade rug to eat breakfast.

Alan laughed again. "*Bapir*, I want handlebars, please."

With a chapped finger, Bapir curled the ends of the yogurt moustache on either side of Alan's puckered-up lips and planted a dab of the stuff on his nose too. Alan collapsed into laughter.

That June morning in 1963, Alan decided that Bapir was the most amusing person on Earth. Perhaps he was the reason Alan adored older people and loved to listen to their stories of *maama rewi*, the trickster coyotes. It hurt Alan that most people with grey hair weren't able to read or write, that their backs hurt, and their papery hands trembled; his dream was to read stories into a loudspeaker for hundreds of elders while they relaxed in a large meadow filled with purple and red flowers.

Grandma brought out more nan, the thin, round bread she had baked in the cylindrical clay oven dug into the basement. Alan made his own "bulletproof" sandwich: fresh honeycomb mixed with ghee. "After I eat this, I can run faster than the bullets," he said.

"Our monkey is growing up, and yet we all treat him as if he is a young child!" Uncle Soran said, making his own bulletproof morsel.

"One's grandchild is always young. That's just how it is." Bapir brushed crumbs from his lap. He winked. "If I were you, Alan, I would make it so I never grew up."

"Growing up is a trap," Grandma agreed, nodding.

"But I like the future," Alan said.

They laughed. Bapir splashed a kiss on Alan's face. "Something a six-year-old would say."

Still wearing his yogurt moustache, Alan frowned. "I am seven."

They cackled.

Father had come to Sulaimani to publish an article he'd written with Uncle Soran illustrating the suffering of the working class in Kurdistan and the rest of Iraq. Kurds had settled in the Zagros Mountains three hundred years before Christ was born, but now Alan's people had no country to call their own. When the Western Allies had drawn the map of the Middle East, they had cut Kurdistan into four pieces, dividing it among Iran, Iraq, Turkey, and Syria.

To visit Bapir with his father, Alan had to ace Kurdish spelling. But Kurdish was not a subject taught at school; Arabic was the only language used there. Father had been trying to teach him and his three brothers to write in their mother tongue, something Alan saw no use for. That morning, Father had skipped breakfast to search the city for a contraband typewriter.

Across the yard, Grandma was watering the pink roses and white lilies. A pounding on the wooden gate in the cement wall that surrounded their plot of land shattered her concentration. She dropped the hose.

"I'll get it." Alan ran across the yard to save her the trouble, but before he reached the gate, six men in Iraqi army uniforms, their faces hidden by striped grey scarves, broke the lock and directed their Kalashnikovs at Grandma's face.

"Where are they?" the shortest one demanded.

Bapir froze, a morsel still in his open mouth. Alan turned to see Uncle Soran leaping over the wall and clambering onto the neighbour's roof.

Somebody — Grandma — grabbed Alan and backed him toward the house.

Nestled against her bosom, Alan watched the soldiers invade the house without waiting for an answer. All six uncles were pulled from their beds or hauled from the bathroom, the basement, a closet, and off the roof next door. Alan wiped off his white handlebars with his sleeve and tried to make sense of the chaos, the jerky movements, the incomprehensible noises escaping people's throats. If only his eyes would give him weapons instead of tears!

His uncles were dragged by the neck, screaming and struggling, like animals to slaughter. Bapir's questions and prayers, Grandma's cries and pleas, the neighbours' screams and curses — nothing had the slightest effect on the soldiers, who conducted the raid without a reply.

Alan's uncles, some still in undershirts, were marched out at gunpoint to army trucks carrying hundreds of Kurdish boys and men between the ages of fourteen and twenty-five. Alan peeled himself from Grandma's arms and ran to the street. The men were told to squat in the beds of the trucks, to place their hands on their heads, and to shut their mouths. Alan looked back at Bapir, who remained next to his smashed gate, head bowed.

Along with other children, women, and the elderly, Alan chased after the lumbering trucks, their huge rubber tires kicking up clouds of dust as they carted away the men amid the anxious cries of the followers. The older men, unarmed and horrified, searched for weapons and ran up the mountains, asking the Peshmerga to come down to the city to face the armed-to-the-teeth soldiers.

Alan trailed after the truck carrying his uncles as it travelled up the hillside at the city centre. His heart had never beaten so fast. The truck finally stopped at the top of the hill, and prisoners were shoved out. On the hard soil, the captives were each given a shovel and ordered to dig.

"*Ebn-al-ghahba*," spat the soldiers — Son of a whore. The angry bystanders were ordered to stand back. People obeyed the AK-47s.

Dirt sprayed over the prisoners' bodies, hair, and eyelashes as their shovels cracked the earth open. Sweat dripped down their faces, and tears ran down over hands that muffled sobs. Alan looked at the pee running down the pants of a boy next to him, at a woman behind him clawing her face and calling out, "God, God, God," at an older man shaking uncontrollably, his hand barely holding on to his crutch. Alan did not seem to be in possession of his own frozen body.

Once the trenches were dug, half of the prisoners were ordered to climb down into the ditches, and the rest were forced to shovel dirt up to their friends' and relatives' chins. Bapir had finally made his way to the top of the hill; he had found Alan in the first row of spectators, gnawing his thumbnail as he watched. Alan begged his grandpa to stop the cruelty.

Bapir hugged him. "They will be released in a few days, these young men." He pressed Alan's head to his chest. "They will be sent back home, *bawanem*, maybe with blisters and bruises, but they will be all right. Pray for them." His hands trembled as he squeezed Alan's. "May it rain before these men die of thirst."

Alan searched through the crowd to find Uncle Soran lifting a pile of dirt with his shovel. Soran's grip loosened when he looked into the eyes of his brother Hewa, whose name meant "hope." Hewa stood in the hole, waiting to be buried by his closest relative, a man whom he'd play-wrestled as a boy and confided in throughout his life.

"Do it, Soran," he said, his eyes shining up from the hole. A bearded soldier dressed in camouflage saw Soran's hesitation. "*Kalb, ebn-al-kalb!*" — Dog, son of a dog — he barked, and swung his Kalashnikov at Soran, the barrel slicing the skin under his left ear.

Soran growled, almost choking, as he turned. With his shovel, he batted the Kalashnikov away so that the gun hit its owner in the head, cutting his scalp. Alan flinched. Bullets rained from every direction. Soran crumbled. His blood sprayed over Hewa, who was screaming and reaching for the perforated body, pulling him forward, pressing his face to the bleeding cheek of his brother.

Crying out, Bapir tried to run toward his sons, but dozens of guns pointed at his chest, dozens of hands held him back. The shower of gunfire wouldn't cease; it struck the hugging siblings, painting them and the soil around them red.

His uncles, still in each other's arms, were buried in one hole. Half of the prisoners were still covered up to their chins with dirt. The remaining ninety-five men were sent down into the other trenches, and the soldiers buried them up to their heads. Alan stared at the rows upon rows of human heads, a garden of agony.

Intoxicated with power, the soldiers kicked the exposed heads of the prisoners, knocked some with the butts of their guns, and jeered at them. At the top of the hill, Bapir sobbed with such force that his wails shook the earth, Alan felt. He clutched Bapir's hunched shoulders and felt impossibly small.

A sunburnt man and a neighbour with shrunken features hugged Bapir, then placed the old man's trembling arms around their shoulders and walked him down the hill.

"Where are my other sons?" Bapir gasped for air.

"Let's get you home," the neighbours told him.

Alan wanted to go with his grandpa, but he was afraid to move. If he took a step, the nightmare would become real. He scanned the hill for his other uncles, who were perhaps buried in some distant trench and unable to move. He couldn't see them. Even Bapir was no longer in sight.

The hubbub was dying down. The strangers who'd witnessed the scene were bound by their dread, their exchanged looks the only solace they could offer each other. Their heads seemed to move in slow motion, as if everyone were suspended underwater. Alan breathed in the atmosphere of quiet horror, of paused hysteria.

Suddenly people cried out in terror. From the road below them, several armoured tanks were approaching. Gaping in disbelief, Alan staggered back, holding a hand to his mouth. He could neither run away nor slow his hammering heart, which was now threatening to explode. When the panicking crowd pushed forward, guns fired into the air to hold them back.

The tanks advanced.

Alan's mind couldn't process the scene before him. Screams. Curses. Pleas. The devilish laughter of the soldiers. He felt an invisible piece of himself drop away and melt into the ground. He was not Alan anymore.

It took an excruciatingly long time for the tanks to pulverize the heads of the prisoners.

The metallic stench of blood, of crushed human flesh and skulls, the foul odour of death made its way into the spectators' nostrils and throats. The lucky ones threw up. Alan did not.

While the giant metal treads ground his family and the other Kurds into nothingness, Alan sucked in shallow and unhelpful breaths.

Bapir lay in bed at home, tossing in anguish, a hand still on his aching chest. By his bedside his wife shed silent tears. Although they had not witnessed the crushing of their sons, they collapsed that day of broken hearts, one after the other. Someone went to find a doctor.

Father arrived at his parents' home oblivious to the tragedy, having taken an unusual road to safeguard his treasure. His typed article was tucked under his shirt. The joy of achievement and hope for his people glowed in his eyes. Then he found his parents on their deathbed. In bits and pieces, the neighbours told him of the massacre, how Ba'ath soldiers — ordered by President Aref and Prime Minister Al-Baker — had punished the Kurds for daring to demand autonomy.

Father ran to the hill, where bewildered children gathered and clung to each other. Beside them, a group of adults wailed and cried, threw dirt into their hair, and beat their faces in terror.

"The British bastards armed Baghdad to kill us. Their tanks, their planes, their goddamn firebombs and mustard gas that killed Iraqis forty years ago are now killing us," Father said to no one in particular.

Then he just stared with unseeing eyes at the gory mound of his pulverized people, his brothers.

Seeing his father's dazed reaction, Alan finally allowed the sobs he'd held in since he first saw the soldiers to burst forth. Other children followed suit. Tears and snot rolled down the dusty faces of the boys and girls who'd been abandoned by the living and dead alike.

Alan ran to his father and held on to his leg. "*Baba gian*, Baba!" he cried. It took a couple of moments before his father noticed him and hugged him close.

"We will leave Iraq. We won't live here any longer." A wild urge to be anywhere but here tugged at Alan's gut too.

Some stoic women and a few elderly men tearlessly buried the unidentifiable remains. They laid down uncarved stones in row after row and asked Alan and the other children to pick wildflowers and pink roses from the slope of the hill, placing them in rows too.

Alan sucked on the blood dripping down his index finger, torn by the rose thorns.

"Alan!" cried a woman whom Alan did not recognize. Three other boys turned when she called; one ran to her. Alan was a popular name, meaning "flag-bearer." It testified to what was expected of the children of a stateless nation, who had to fight against nonexistence.

Gezahegn Mekonnen Demissie
(Ethiopia)

GEZAHEGN MEKONNEN DEMISSIE is an Ethiopian journalist and filmmaker, one of the founding members of PEN Ethiopia, and Executive Director of Bridge Entertainment. He currently lives in Toronto, Canada, where he publishes the community journal, and radio show/podcast, *New Perspective* አዲስ ቅኝት. He is a current board member and the leader of PEN Canada's Writers-in-Exile community.

Born in Addis Ababa, Gezahegn obtained a degree in global studies, international relations, and literature. He directed and produced several documentaries, two feature films, and produced a TV series on urban culture and architecture in Addis Ababa. He worked for different print and broadcast media outlets in Ethiopia before establishing his own magazines, newspapers, and radio shows. All of these were shut down by the repressive Ethiopian government. He came to Canada in 2015 and has continued to develop projects about Ethiopia and the immigrant experience in exile. *Tizita* is his first short documentary for CBC Short Docs, which was produced in collaboration with Canadian production companies Primitive Entertainment and Rhombus Media. In 2019 he received the National Ethnic Press and Media Council of Canada Award for providing exceptional journalism to the Ethiopian Community, and in 2021 he and his media, *New Perspective* አዲስበቅኝት, received a community Champion award from Arif Varani, MP for Parkdale–High Park in Toronto.

The Tale of My Two Countries
Autobiographical Play

Prologue

IN THE BEGINNING was the Word. And the Word was in me. I later learned that there is no life without the Word, but the Word is a solid foundation that balances both my spirit and my body. Mankind is nothing but a word.

I am here now. I was there yesterday. But I am the same yesterday and today. I will continue to live after tomorrow. But my existence continues to persist on a verbal basis.

I came to life today instead of yesterday. I was dust yesterday, today I am flesh. Tomorrow I will be dust. I will return from whence I came. I was Ethiopian yesterday and today I am Canadian; tomorrow I will be in heaven. But I am all of these things and in all of these states. I have the words that give them all meaning.

What does it mean, being Ethiopian yesterday and being Canadian today? What did I lose as an Ethiopian? What did I gain by becoming a Canadian? What has the changed name of my nationality changed in my identity? What is missing? Where am I in these two worlds, and what is the difference between yesterday and today?

The main purpose of this brief self-image analysis is to try to see and understand differences in myself and between my selves, today, in different settings. A change of act in drama implies not only a change of time and place but also a changed complexity of action. Where am I left as a character after the act has changed? What effect did the change have on me?

To illustrate the truth of Shakespeare's claim that the world is a drama, I would like to present my short life-experience in two acts. Of course, the length of my act may increase or decrease, but human life is a wonderful play and mine has been no exception. We all are the actors upon a stage. If we are lucky, our lives will be comedic, and we will be assigned to laughter, joy, and happiness. If not, we will live in a world of both sadness and happiness, as in a tragicomedy. Or we may not have choice and will leave the drama; we may be written out of the script! In my case though, I won't depart the stage without first explaining myself. I invite you into my drama and respectfully request that you give me your attention while the curtain is raised, and the theatre lights go out.

(The lights go out. The curtain is raised.)

ACT ONE
SCENE ONE

When the Veil Is Revealed
(Light goes on)

My homeland is like a fatherland to me, although many prefer to call it a motherland. When I read the history of my homeland, from ancient times to the current time, it is full of chaos. Thus, I prefer to consider my second home to be my motherland; it is quiet and orderly. My fatherland taught me to be proud of myself and, as an African, proud of not being colonized. My second country, my new home, has shown me hospitality, kindness, respect for rights, forgiveness, and order.

    I was born in a middle-class family, by Ethiopian standards. My father was a well-known designer and tailor. He owned a big store in the middle of the main market in Addis Ababa. He did well, but when Haile Selassie was overthrown, Dad was considered bourgeois by the cadres of the military junta. My mother was born and raised in the northern provinces of Ethiopia. She was a daughter of a major who was a member of the royal border guard. Her father's role meant that, in her youth, she travelled through different parts of the country, and as a result, she learned to speak many languages. I remember her speaking Tigrigna, Oromo, Afar, and Amharic. This ability helped her to learn about and understand the diversity of Ethiopian culture and the complexity of Ethiopian identity. This had a profound influence on me and on my siblings, helping us to have a broader, pan-ethnic understanding of our Ethiopian nation. My mother was my inspiration for storytelling and imaginative exploration.

I was born in the mid-70s in the middle of the Cold War. Globally it may have been a "cold" period, but it was not a cool time in Ethiopia where, in a matrix of ideological differences, conflict through a war of attrition had broken out between different ethnic groups. My country of birth dates its origin back 3,000 years to when it was the throne of St. David and King Solomon. The last emperor of this long-reigning dynasty, Haile Selassie, was overthrown (only recently, in historic terms) by a military junta called the Derg. I was born into the so-called socialist-military system of that time, just ten months after the Derg took power. Since that time, Ethiopia has been in turmoil.

My childhood began in Addis Ababa in the neighbourhood of General Wingate, which was named after a British officer who came to Ethiopia via Sudan in 1941, leading a British army to reinstate Haile Selassie back to his throne.

Growing up in the Wingate neighbourhood, I thought about the second Ethiopian-Italian War and asked myself about the complexities of power struggles around the world. The British Council Library at the General Wingate High School helped to open my eyes in this regard. As a teenager, when I went to the library, the Russian teachers "reminded" me that Ethiopia was "a shipwreck between the West and the East." We were not allowed to talk or read about Western culture, or its literature and philosophy; it was a time when the military junta was criticizing Western culture as a "bourgeois" culture. We were surrounded by Soviet literature inspired by socialist realism. All the library books written by the British, American, and other Western writers were put aside, hidden at the back of the library shelves. But I was able to read them when nobody was looking. The library was my escape from that monotonous time.

Although the world paid little attention to my first country, Ethiopia, a lot happened there in the mid-70s — and a lot is still happening even now. My childhood was full of contradictory things.

Most of the city's graveyards were in the neighbourhood where I grew up. Inevitably and on a daily basis, I observed the interactions of life and death.

The elementary school I attended was surrounded by graveyards. There was a graveyard for the poor who died with no family relations, a graveyard for the orthodox Christians, and a graveyard for Catholics and non-Ethiopians. We played in the graveyards, particularly that of the poor, every day. We picked up human skeletons that we saw in and around the pits and compared them to the skeletons we saw in our textbooks. In truth, I was terrified. My friends held the skeletons, but I did not touch them; my mother had warned me not to go to the cemetery! Some of the dead were buried in a portion of a graveyard that was a beautiful park. It was right in front of Wingate School. When the wealthy came in their cars for funerals at the graveyard, children would earn pennies by watching over the cars to keep them safe.

This situation has always reminded me of a scene in Shakespeare's play *Hamlet* when Hamlet picks up the skull of a childhood friend at the cemetery and says:

Dust is earth, of earth we make loam. And why, of that loam
whereto he was converted, might they not stop a beer barrel?
Imperious Caesar, dead and turned to clay,
Might stop a hole to keep the wind away.
Oh, that that earth which kept the world in awe
Should patch a wall t'expel the winter's flaw!

As we grew from our childhood to our youth, a change of government took place in Ethiopia. The change was a result of the end of the Cold War.

As this change of government occurred and I thought about that place where I played — the graveyard — I thought of the bones of young people who had died because of their political beliefs; their bones were put in the pits and graves where we used to play.

SCENE TWO

(Light goes on)

Another Turning Point

1991 (1983 in the Ethiopian calendar) was a year of milestones — not just for me, but for my homeland, Ethiopia.

The collapse of the Soviet Union, which had existed for seventy years, had a significant impact on Ethiopia, which had gone through a seventeen-year-long civil war with Eritrean secessionists and their Tigrayan partners. The Russian collapse brought about another change — this one in Ethiopia. The military government in Ethiopia was replaced by a tribal and guerrilla government. Ethiopia was under the control of another horrible regime, one that claimed to have produced the liberation from the former leftist-socialist state. This new government (and system) was hated by Ethiopians. However, it was blessed by the West. The ethnic, apartheid-based political system of this regime implemented the tribal/ethnic federalism that is still plaguing Ethiopia today.

It was during this time, a time of major change, that I graduated from elementary to high school.

As I grew into my adolescent years, Ethiopia moved into the unknown.

In a period of free expression and free press that the new government allowed — in order to deceive its Western allies (to look democratic) I began to write poems and stories. This activity opened the door for my future career as a journalist. However, the government, which since its inception had been hostile to the media and to journalists, made it clear that journalism was not a welcome profession. But my attitudes had been formed; I would commit myself to study at the school of journalism. Professionally, I could go nowhere else! I started speaking out for freedom of expression and true journalism, even before I was a full-time journalist.

Recognition that I received in the literary competitions in which I had participated while still in high school paved the way to my future career.

At that time, there were two options for anyone who wanted to fight for rights in Ethiopia. One: embrace the gun. Two: engage in peaceful struggle. Peaceful struggle had two forms. One was with the pen. The other was through a peaceful struggle to become a member of a political party. I chose the pen. The "word" was definitely in me; I chose to share the word with others.

SCENE THREE

The Beginning of a Life of Journalism

With the advent of the new millennium, my journalistic career began. I started as a reporter and columnist for the *Addis Ababa City Gazette*. Starting my career there laid a great foundation for my subsequent journalistic career. Working as a journalist in the time of an anti-journalistic government, I became familiar with the political structure of the bureaucracy and the system's approach to the media. As a columnist, I was penalized many times for articles I wrote. Salary cuts and suspension of my column were my frequent punishments. Despite these things, I did not hesitate to write the truth. As a result, I got the nickname "እንደልቡ" — "Unafraid." I was deprived of employment benefits and of wage increases. I was told by my colleagues that I could have had a car and a promotion and a house if I had obeyed the orders of my superiors — if I had written what they wanted. But I refused.

In this job, under such conditions, it became difficult to keep up a non-stop war every day. So, I opened my own film production initiative. I was able to sell my movie scripts — if only for a pittance — and I produced and directed two films. These activities, however, made me seem rebellious in the eyes of my superiors.

In 2005, a few months before the national election, I entered the free market. Using the initial capital I had produced from my film career, I launched *New Beauty* አዲስ ውበት magazine.

That year, 2005, was memorable, not only in my life but also for many Ethiopians. But it was not memorable for good things. The day after the 2005 election, the free press in Ethiopia was completely shut down — including my new magazine. This was the beginning of a challenging period for me as a freelance journalist.

However, during that very challenging time, I found my life partner, Sosina. This occurred when I was publishing my "shut-down" magazine. Sosina was working as a columnist for the *New Beauty* magazine. Our relationship grew and the day after the magazine actually closed, we joined forces in another media project.

In 2005, as a result of the crackdown on rival political parties and on the independent press, the government's false face was revealed, and their Western friends saw the true nature of the regime.

It was at this time that the creation of PEN Ethiopia was suggested. PEN is an international literary and human rights organization. The arrival in Addis Ababa of a Norwegian professor and vice president of PEN Norway, Elizabeth Eddi, stimulated the impetus for PEN Ethiopia.

My wife, Sosina Ashenafi, and I continued our journey together by becoming part of this international organization. There was no free speech and no free media in Ethiopia, so the idea of establishing a branch of PEN in Ethiopia gave us great hope.

I was sent by PEN International to Sierra Leone for an exchange of experiences with colleagues there. It was after returning from Sierra Leone that I and my friends set out on a mission to establish PEN Ethiopia. I became an active participant in PEN International and a founding member of PEN Ethiopia.

Not surprisingly, the government tried to make PEN look bad.

After we established PEN Ethiopia, our organization held three international congresses in Addis Ababa. This, of course, focused the government's attention on our activities. Repressive laws had been enacted in Ethiopia following the election. Two of them particularly affected us: the "media law" and the draconian "non-governmental organizations" (NGOs) law, which drastically restricted our activities and prevented us from receiving more than ten per cent of any aid or assistance that we might receive from outside the country. Despite these impediments, we did our best to inform Ethiopian journalists and the public (as wisely as possible) about the abductions and abuses in that were occurring. Government agents began to follow us and, using different means, harass us.

The focus of our third PEN congress, in 2014, was freedom of expression and literature in Ethiopia. It included guests from Turkey, Britain, Norway, South Africa, Italy, and other countries as well as Ethiopian journalists, writers, and philosophers who were outraged by the dictatorship in Ethiopia. The government paid close attention to this event as it coincided with the sixth national election. Following that third and final congress, we, the four board members of PEN Ethiopia, became concerned for our safety, and in October 2015 felt compelled to leave our country.

ACT TWO
SCENE ONE
(The curtain opens)

Québec City, Canada

In the fall of 2015, I, Gezahegn Mekonnen Demissie, the board secretary of PEN Ethiopia, as well as the president, Solomon Hailemariam, the vice president, Dejene Tesema, and board member, Aschalew Kebede, arrived in Québec City, Canada, to attend the 81st annual congress of PEN International.

Members of PEN International and PEN Québec welcomed us warmly. It was the fall season in Canada and the trees were turning yellow, preparing for the coming winter; I wondered what the future might hold for us as we contemplated our destiny. The main members of the PEN International Board of Trustees were present to attend the organization's General Assembly. To that board, we Ethiopians explained what PEN Ethiopia had gone through and the dangers we were facing. The board gave us advice and as a result we chose to stay here in Canada rather than die in Ethiopia.

With this momentous decision having been made, immediately we were confronted with the question: "Where can we stay?" I realized that this new scene was not going to be easy — leaving my family and Ethiopia, the country where I was born and raised, to live in Canada.

I remember our short flight from Québec City to Toronto after the congress. It was different from our trip from Ethiopia to Canada. The trip to Toronto was short, but I did not know where I was going. The journey from Ethiopia to Canada was long, but at least I had known my destination — Canada. Upon arrival at Pearson Airport in Toronto, we went to pick up our luggage before we were to be taken into the city by people connected with PEN. But there was a sudden shock. I was saddened to learn that the airline had not been notified about my changed plan. I would disembark in Toronto, but my suitcase had been processed for return to Ethiopia.

My immediate concern and priority, however, was to find a place to stay.

On the way into Toronto, a couple connected to PEN — Grace and Peter — told us that the four of us from Ethiopia would be divided into two groups and that we would be staying in different places. After driving from the airport to the city centre, the first house we were taken to was for Solomon and Aschalew. The woman who received them, barefoot at her door, was unknown to us, but when she saw that we had arrived, she opened her door and expressed welcome. That woman was CBC's Joan Leishman. Since that moment, we have seen that reception as an example of typical refugee welcome in Canada.

My friend Dejene Tesema and I were destined to go to another house, that of a great writer and filmmaker couple, Keith and Mary Young Leckie. When Keith received us, his wife, Mary, was away for a film shoot, but he and their three dogs warmly welcomed us. He served food he had bought from an Ethiopian restaurant as well as a Kenyan-tasting beer. This made us feel that we had been invited into an Ethiopian home.

We spent the first night talking about Canadian history and literature and about the situation in Ethiopia. Keith gave us a detailed account of the election campaign that was underway in Canada at that time. I noted that in Ethiopia, just days after a contested election, the ruling party had declared a one hundred per cent victory but that in comparison, Canada was about to peacefully send out the nine-year government of Stephen Harper and welcome a new Liberal government under Justin Trudeau.

We lodged for two days in the upper-level room provided to us in Keith's house. I felt like I was a newborn chick in a nest just after the hatching of its egg. I sat in the upstairs lounge and looked outside, thinking about my future. I saw people walking down an asphalt road through "the village." I did not know where that narrow road could possibly lead us, but from the window that I peered through, I could see it was a different world. I felt inhibited; I felt I could not leave that room to meet or greet anyone. But I knew that in situations like this, when one feels no hope, it was only natural to wonder about one's new future (mine in Canada) and to wonder about the people on whom I was now dependent: who these people were who were unreservedly welcoming us, showing us that there could be light at end of the darkness?

After two days with Keith Leckie, we learned that we were going to move to another house. The night we moved was that of the Canadian election, so everywhere there was only talk about that and about the 25,000 Syrian refugees Canada had committed to accept, all of whom were expected to come to Canada very soon. We four Ethiopian journalists-refugees felt insignificant compared to 25,000 Syrian refugees that Canada would receive. However, we were warmly welcomed by Mary Jo Leddy, then chair of Writers-in Exile and co-founder of Romero House, a refugee settlement centre in Toronto.

That evening, Keith took us to the home of Lisa Clarkson and her family. Lisa stood at the door and, with her daughter Lucy, welcomed us. Their house had been modified by Lisa and her family so as to be able to accept Syrian refugees. However, due to a delay in the arrival of those refugees, space was available for us. My friend Dejene and I thus had a place to rest, a new home. Lisa's reception was warming for a man who had left behind his beloved wife and child and had lost all his clothes and luggage.

SCENE TWO

The Beginnings of Canadian Life

When our lives began in Canada, our childhood years seemed to be many years behind us. Now, new to Canada, everything was immediate. Our new Canadian friends kept constant and close watch over every aspect of our well-being: what there was for us to eat, the winter clothing we needed to wear, and how we should use our time. Liz, Alison, Paola, Breana, Katelin, Valentin, Hannah, Mathew, and Jane, and all the people connected to the Romero House will never be forgotten. The host who received Solomon was Caroline (and her boyfriend Michael). They and many other people played very special roles during our early days in Canada.

When I think of those early months here, it seems that they were like the first few months of a baby's life in the hands of caring parents. Or perhaps we had the experience of newlyweds: we were "on a honeymoon."

Christmas and Getting Acquainted with Canadian Culture and Ways of Life

The fall season was over. Winter was approaching. But the months before our first winter in Canada had been "warm"; we found ourselves in a climate of friendship. This period of time allowed us to get to know more about Canadian culture and life. Our first Canadian Christmas dinner was hosted by our friend, the then president of PEN International, Dr. John Ralston Saul and by his wife, the Rt. Honourable Adrienne Clarkson, renowned journalist and former governor general of Canada. These two distinguished Canadians had been PEN Ethiopia's guests of honour, in February 2012, at the inauguration of PEN Ethiopia in Addis Ababa. They had remained friends of PEN Ethiopia from day one. During the holiday period, in addition to a dinner at a Chinese restaurant, we also attended our first cinema where we were thrilled to watch the new Star Wars film. As I recall those Christmas events, I remember Marian Botsford who invited us to the Yorkminster Park Baptist Church to hear Handel's choral masterpiece, *Messiah*, performed by the Mendelssohn Choir. It was at that concert that we got to know a new friend, Keith Powell, who had recently returned from a visit to Ethiopia with his family. That trip had been an unforgettable experience for him; a relationship with us was a great chance for him to continue to have a connection with Ethiopia. Keith has taken us to various places in and around Toronto and, with his family, has helped us to become familiar with our new environment and the Canadian way of living.

The End of the Honeymoon and the Coming of Responsibility

As 2016 began, our focus was on starting our new lives. Our immigration case was heard and decided in February. Under Canadian refugee law and the International Convention on Refugees, we had become "Convention refugees" and "protected" persons. This convention effectively guaranteed our status. We were officially granted refugee status in Canada, and with this status we could apply to bring our families to Canada. The success of this process was greatly enhanced by the contributions of John Ralston Saul and Adrienne Clarkson, Lisa Clarkson, Keith and Mary Young Leckie, Mary Jo Leddy and Romero House, PEN Canada, and our friends. These friends and advocates have been a great help at every step along the way, assisting us with the big tasks and with the nitty-gritty ones, like how to fill out the official forms required by our lawyer. PEN Canada subsequently provided us some money from an emergency fund to cover the cost of our applications for family reunification. After all of our applications for official status had been approved by the Immigration Board, our friends and associates gathered and welcomed us at a bright celebratory party at the Romero House. Dr. Ralston Saul recalled the welcome he had received from us during his visit to Addis Ababa and spoke to the community members and guests about the importance of PEN Ethiopia and about our contributions to freedom of expression.

The next step, after we received official status, was to find jobs and to be self-sufficient. For my part, I tried to learn how the media and entertainment industry worked in Canada and about how the country's laws impact newcomers. I started my Canadian career by spending some time in various forums, networking and promoting my previous work, and, thanks to Hannah Fisher, a friend I'd made through PEN Canada, I attended the Toronto International Film Festival. My networking experience greatly helped me to understand the media sector. And I am grateful to John Ralston Saul, who played a major role in guiding me in the film industry, a contribution that I will never forget.

I met two Canadian production companies, and Niv Fichman and Kevin McMahon. Their friendship was unforgettable. As a result of these connections, a proposal I submitted to make three films was accepted. One of these documentaries was filmed with the support of both the production companies and the Canadian Broadcasting Corporation. My first experience of making a movie with the CBC helped pave the way for me to start my media career with Ethiopians and Canadians in Toronto.

I enjoyed another special opportunity in 2015: my participation in the annual Ethiopian Sports Festival in North America, which would be held in Toronto the following year. I hosted an event at the festival and participated in the production. My involvement gave me an opportunity to film an on-stage commemoration of the work of Girma Cheru, an Ethiopian sport and television presenter who now lived in Toronto. I included this commemoration in a documentary I was making about Girma.

These involvements, in turn, gave me opportunities to meet directly with members of the Ethiopian community in Toronto.

SCENE THREE

Establishment of a New Newspaper

Setting up a newspaper in a new country, and managing a media initiative, is a challenge. It is especially challenging to create a diaspora newspaper that is relevant and credible to a community that is divided along ethnic and political lines.

I realized that there were people who had tried to publish an Ethiopian-Canadian newspaper before me who had had to stop publishing and that there was also one long-standing publication that was not respected by the community because it lacked expertise. Despite these discouraging precedents and, in strategic response to them, I decided to publish a new newspaper with a broad reach. This decision required me to rethink my career and reconsider my political perspective.

This initiative and the challenges that came with it — publishing, distribution, advertising, and so on — were too great for me to handle alone. If my wife had not been by my side, helping professionally in so many ways, my life in Canadian media would have been short-lived. I also received support from a number of my fellow Ethiopian countrypeople. The Ethiopian community here has been and still is a great source of motivation, partnership, and encouragement to me. Additionally, I received support from my fellow countrypeople, the Canadians.

Journalism is a challenge in a new country. But the challenge here in Canada is insignificant compared to the challenge that existed in Ethiopia. The key to journalism and media work is freedom of expression and legal protection. My beliefs and desires about these things made me want to get into my chosen career here in Canada. The persecution I endured in Ethiopia has led me to consider my journalism circumstances in the two countries as having been as different as hell and heaven. More than three media outlets that I established in Ethiopia had been directly or indirectly suppressed by the repressive and hostile government there. Here in Canada, although it is not a trivial matter to keep a media outlet working and to keep it afloat financially, I have realized my dream of starting my own media company and of establishing a free media initiative. I respect the Canadian legal system for treating everyone equally.

When I got a licence in 2017, under the auspices of Bridge Entertainment, to establish my *New Perspective* አዲስ ቅኝት newspaper, I dreamed of more than just publishing a newspaper — I also dreamed of publishing books and of producing films. But the newspaper's work did not initially go as easily or smoothly as I thought it would. My wife Sosina, at that point still in Ethiopia, was writing for my *New Perspective* newspaper there. Ethiopian government spies here in Canada were aware of our work and of our criticisms. Knowing that my family was in Ethiopia and that their lives could be put in danger by what I wrote here, I was fearful about speaking honestly and telling truths. Sosina and I discussed these matters: she was solidly supportive that we carry on with honest journalism.

To get my media initiative established, I went around to the businesses in our community, promoting the establishment of my newspaper, explaining the importance of community media, and seeking financial support. Sometimes the business owners hid when they saw me coming. A number of people advised me not to pursue the notion of a newspaper because they believed that a considerable amount of subsidy money was already being provided for media and art in Canada. I, however, did not even know where such money came from or how it flowed. Nevertheless, a few people who were aware of my efforts gave me good direction and generous and much-needed support.

It was only when I was about to start the newspaper that I began to consider that newspapers here in Canada would likely have their own professional association, since freedom of thought and association seem infinite in this country. I searched Google and found out that there was an Ontario Newspaper Publishers Association with an office based in Toronto. As soon as the first edition of my newspaper was published here, I went straight to that office with a copy. A woman I met — if I am not mistaken, the CEO — told me that there was also yet another association, one that was particularly suitable for my type of newspaper: the National Ethnic Press and Media Council of Canada. At her suggestion, I went to that association's office in Toronto. The association's president, Thomas Saras, politely welcomed me and registered me as a member. Since then, I have attended regular monthly meetings, with all the members, to discuss our newspapers and media issues. In 2019, I received a Special Journalism Award from this association.

My newspaper, *New Perspective/Addis Kignit* አዲስ ቅኝት was up and running. And for thirty months it continued to run and be produced in hard copy. That is when the COVID-19 epidemic hit — at which time, in view of the changed circumstances, I opened a new website and converted the newspaper into a digital publication.

2018 The Arrival of My Family: Feeling Relief

For almost three years, as a refugee in Canada, I had spent a lot of time alone without my family. My wife and my son in Ethiopia longed for me and I longed for them. My son also wondered what I would expect of them when eventually they arrived in Canada.

My agony of loneliness in this new country, although acute, was not unendurable because I had a family that I loved and that I knew loved me, and because I had Canadian friends who, although new in my life and new to my challenges and my ordeal, were both supportive and optimistic about my application for family reunification.

As the Ethiopian New Year approached, my wife and my son, Hyssop, arrived in Canada. I went to Toronto's Pearson Airport with Lisa and her family to receive them. However, due to political turmoil in Ethiopia, the flight from Addis Ababa had been delayed. For three hours we waited, not knowing the reason for the delay or if the plane would actually arrive. Lisa and her husband, Gordy, and their children, Henry and Lucy, hung out with me for those excruciating three hours. When my wife and son finally came out of the arrivals doorway, I began to cry. They looked haggard and I felt miserable for them. I also felt guilty that my life choices had forced them to suffer so much. They, in turn, saw the misery in my face, the suffering that I was experiencing. They were alarmed and appalled. But then I suddenly jumped up and ran to them.

SCENE FOUR

Settling In and Feeling Whole

The arrival of my wife and partner opened a new chapter in my life. We started a weekly radio program: I was keen to see her continue her radio career, which she had loved and worked at for many years in Ethiopia. Our *New Perspective* አዲስ ቀኝት program, online on Radio Regent, focused on immigration and its effect on women, on the news and current affairs, and on the arts. It attracted the attention of the Ethiopian community and a large audience. The COVID-19 epidemic interrupted our live weekly radio programing from the Radio Regent studio. Unable to work from the studio, we began live streaming a podcast, interviewing people by Zoom. This led to the launch of our YouTube channel for *New Perspective*. During the two-plus years of the COVID-19 pandemic, our YouTube channel became popular. We hosted and interviewed guests from all over the world, including Ethiopia, and have continued to do so. We have spoken to more than two hundred writers, journalists, community leaders, politicians, religious people, and professionals in both Amharic and English.

We are now preparing to launch e-commerce marketing through which we will sell audiovisual material and books from a variety of creators that focus on Ethiopian and African issues. There are so many ways to share the word.

Endpiece Soliloquy

Canada was once, for me, a make-believe land, a faraway place that was like a dream. I came here aware of the opportunities that could exist but also aware of this land's problems — such as the appalling history of its treatment of indigenous peoples and the unresolved issues that remain to this day, and the existence of systemic racism. But I came here, and I am here, determined to be a part of the solution to this country's problems. Not everything is perfect. I have faced barriers and discrimination and I will face these issues again. But we will work together to address the problems. We are not discouraged in Canada because for us, Canada is a marriage that has given us rebirth and a second chance.

I believe in Canadian society — a society that is more advanced and progressive than its political systems. Ethiopia had problems in the political realm but also at the societal level. Society here in Canada is enlightened. It is welcoming and, for the most part, not judgmental.

This provides better prospects for making a future; not a perfect future — it can't be made perfect — but a better future. One that will, perhaps, be close to perfect.

I see a future that is better than the past, a future for me that will be better than my past. I am happy to see that future here.

(The lights go down but not out. The curtain is drawn, as if to close but, it stays open)

Curtain Call

(The house lights are on. The players come out. The spotlights come up and strains of Leonard Cohen's "Hallelujah" are heard.)

The players, each and every player who has appeared in the script, all stand together and face the audience. They speak good cheer and good luck to each other and to all who have attended.

The playwright comes to the front of the stage. He thanks each player for the part they have played in his drama. He thanks them for their good will. And he concludes with only "Hallelujah" on his lips.

Arzu Yildiz
(Turkey)

ARZU YILDIZ is a Turkish-born, award-winning investigative journalist, senior reporter, editor, public speaker, and author of four books. She built a career at the liberal, democratic daily *Taraf* newspaper where she reported on human rights issues, corruption, and illegal gun trafficking. Jailed and stripped of legal guardianship of her children for reporting on the trial of state prosecutors, Yildiz spent five months in hiding after a government crackdown on press freedom before fleeing to Canada via Greece.

"I take every step for refugees who are in despair anywhere in the world, and I tell them we must move forward!" Yildiz was the recipient of the 2021 PEN Canada-Humber College Writers-in-Exile Scholarship. She is featured in Canadian filmmaker James Cullingham's 2021 documentary *The Cost of Freedom*. She has an MA in Creative Writing from the University of Gloucestershire.

INTRODUCTION

The country of Turkey was founded on October 29, 1923, under the leadership of Mustafa Kemal Atatürk, after the collapse of the Ottoman Empire. Turkey, whose population is predominantly Muslim, is the only secular country among Muslim countries. Geographically, it is a bridge between Asia and Europe. Kurds form the majority of the population in the east of the country, and Turks in the west and middle of the country. The official language is Turkish. The assimilation policies towards minorities and the fact that Kurdish and other languages were not accepted as official languages prevented the establishment of democratic rule in the country. After the country's founding, the army often intervened in politics, continuing the coup tradition and changing the power structure by undemocratic means. Soldiers executed a duly elected prime minister in 1961.

Turkey has borders with Syria, Iraq, Iran, Armenia, Georgia, Greece, and Bulgaria. Since it is located between Europe and Asia, trafficking of people, drugs, and weapons is common. Mafia and deep state problems could not be resolved in Turkey. Nearly 18,000 unsolved murders remain on the books. Massacres in regions where minorities live have never been investigated. According to official figures, five million refugees live in Turkey. Almost four million of them are Syrian refugees. In addition, it receives immigrants from Afghanistan, Iran, Iraq, and some African countries. On December 5, 1934, women were granted the right to vote and be elected. In the last sixty years, coups, restricted freedom of the press, and government intervention in the judiciary have prevented Turkey from experiencing full democracy. Between 2013 and 2021, it ranked as one of the top three countries for violations of freedom of the press. The European Court of Human Rights determined that Turkey had the most violations of rights regarding fair trial. According to the data of 2022, Turkey ranks seventh among the countries with the highest number of prisoners in the world, with 291,198.

What if Geography Is Your Destiny?

AS A REBELLIOUS young girl in Turkey, I did not nurture any future plans, such as becoming educated, immersing myself in a vocation, or working in a gainful job. For me, it was enough to survive the violence and rebellion in a patriarchal society. I was not a good person when I bullied others by withholding free passes for people to enter the park in my neighbourhood. I was playing soccer, doing tae kwon do, and boxing. At midnight I was aimlessly wandering in the streets like a vagabond, cigarette in my hand. On some of these occasions I got sleepy and took a nap in the park. One evening when I arrived home I was confronted by my curious mother at the door. She told me to stay at home in the evenings. Defiantly, I demanded to know why she was asking me to report my whereabouts. (In my view, nobody, including my mom, could interrogate me.) I was back out on the street the next night.

At home, I watched all the matches of Hamza Yerlikaya — an Olympic gold medallist in wrestling — and learned the art of the sport. I even beat men in wrestling; I was living more like a boy than a girl. While many kids summoned their brothers when shit happened in a fight, my four brothers called me, their sister, for help.

One day when I was a freshman, I was returning home from high school. We lived in a residential area used by the active-duty personnel of the military and their families.

I saw a book in a trash bin at the corner of the street near our home. The book had no cover. I grabbed the book (it was free, after all) and went home. When I retreated to my room after sunset, I began to read this book with no front page.

It was a poetry book called *Sea of Sorrows* by Ümit Yaşar Oğuzcan. I was so moved by the book that I bought another poetry book called *What If You Are Not at Home* by Cemal Safi.

Then books by Ahmed Arif and Nâzım Hikmet. When my mother discovered my devouring of poetry books, she demanded, "Are you in love?" as if being in love were the only thing that would inspire someone to read poetry. My mother had never read books like these.

I now loved reading books and poems, but I was not in love.

Meanwhile, my outcast life continued unchanged. Because of the impression my unusual style conveyed, nobody could picture me reading books at night. The majority of people judge a book by the cover; they judge you based on what they see and what they hear about you. People never judge according to what is inside you. Instead, they judge you by what they see.

At this time, there was someone who fell for me. But his mother was dead set against me. She declared, "I would never want that girl! She is a mischief-maker, and she would corrupt you. She wanders with a tomato in her hand." (I still enjoy tomato sandwiches.) In her view, I was someone who should be avoided.

At school, people's chattering about college never captured my interest or attention. At night, I was used to reading any book that I got. And yet, despite these being hurly-burly days, and despite my lack of interest in post-secondary schooling, I took the university entrance exam. It wasn't something I'd put a lot of thought or preparation into, and I only took the test out of curiosity after I heard that there was such an exam. Much to my surprise, I got perfect scores in the literature and social sciences parts. The books devoured during those nights seemed to have compensated for my lack of proper, planned study. When I saw the results, I decided to go to university, though at the time I didn't intend to study journalism. In the selection and enrollment process, I selected the law department as my first choice, and just randomly added journalism as my second choice.

But I was amazed to be admitted to the Journalism Department of Istanbul-based Bilgi University.

"Let's see what it is about, and I can hang out in Istanbul," was my motto when I set out to live in Turkey's largest city. When I left Ankara, even our neighbours were shocked and told my mother that they didn't believe I would finish university. They didn't think I had the good profile of a university student.

The first lecture was with an academic named Okan Tanşu. In his introduction to journalism, he told us, "Whoever wants to be a journalist in this class should go out after this lecture and seek an internship opportunity today. Forget money. Get a job in a small, independent media outlet. You cannot freely report at a corporate media company, as there would be an overriding concern for advertising revenue. You should be seeking truth when you are real, honest journalists."

When I left the lecture, I went to the studio of *32nd Day* (a popular national television program that had a studio branch at Istanbul Bilgi University) to talk about an internship opportunity. They accepted me the very same day.

At this time, I was going to one campus to study journalism and the second campus for my minor in history, all while working on my internship five days a week. I was also used to going to bars three nights a week. I got accustomed to living on three hours of sleep a day.

As well, I had a lover in Ankara.

"A job can be found, but not a husband," I thought. Four years later, I returned to Ankara when I had graduated from college. (Now I realize it would have been okay if I hadn't had a lover after all.)

"First get a job, then get married," my father told me.

I said to myself that if I followed the advice of my father, I would marry after menopause. But my life is mine. So, I got married.

Meanwhile, six months earlier, I had gone with a friend to the first play of the Pink Life Association, which was being staged by transgender people in Istanbul. There I saw a young woman taking pictures. She was a journalist for sure, but I couldn't help but wonder what media outlet would deploy a reporter to follow such a play. Was Turkey really that progressive?

I decided to ask her.

"The *Taraf Daily*," she said.

This was a new newspaper to me, and I wondered who else worked there. She listed the staff. One of them was Ahmet Altan, the son of Çetin Altan. I was a loyal reader of the father, who was a famous journalist and writer with countless books to his name. It was enough for me that his son worked at the *Taraf Daily*.

Later, I talked about what I'd learned with a friend; we agreed this was the newspaper I must work for.

I went to the office of the *Taraf Daily* when I returned to Ankara. My first challenge was to try to be seen at a newspaper office without references from powerful people. I had nothing of the sort. I thought of a reference from my father, but while he was an intellectual, he was an intellectual construction worker, and I was certain a reference from a construction worker wouldn't carry the day.

"I am working on a master's thesis, and I would like to meet with the editor," I said as I entered the office.

Lale Kemal had recently become the new editor.

I explained when we met: "When I entered, I lied about the master's thesis. I just want to work here. I do not want money. And if you don't hire me now, I'll keep coming every morning until you do." She didn't say anything.

The next morning, with no job offer, I did as promised, and went and started working there without pay. Two months later, Ahmet Altan, who was our Istanbul office's chief editor, assigned me to work at the court-house.

When I started as a reporter at the courthouse, I had no information about the affairs of the courthouse and courts. I entered the press room, where there were reporters from many different newspapers. When I told them I was from *Taraf* they said I should not be in the room at any time, and that I would not even be given a key.

It was a typical display of prejudice and tribalism. I wanted no part of it, and for a long time, I did not enter the press room.

Originally, I had wanted to study law at university, maybe to become a lawyer or prosecutor, but as a twist and irony of fate, I had ended up entering the courthouse as a judicial reporter. Being on the beat for long stints and staying in the court halls longer than anyone else allowed me to break the news on a number of occasions.

For many people, *Taraf* was the newspaper that covered the high-profile Ergenekon and Balyoz deep state trials; for me it was the taboo-breaking and revolutionary newspaper that had sent a reporter to the Pink Life Association's play.

In that courthouse, I saw a mother whose son was a killer, and I saw another mother whose son had been killed. And some cases of rapes of little children. And I heard how so-called pious people bribed others in massage parlours. The downtrodden had their stories: real, unusual, painful, and often cruel.

Sometimes I ended up sleeping there. Often, I did not go home for two days at a time.

I worked as a courthouse reporter for so many years that I never thought what kind of ideology a judicial member subscribes to. I would never grasp other people's mindsets of over-analyzing people's motives, intentions, and personal beliefs. Besides studying files at night, I read dozens of law books and watched movies and documentaries.

My story was not limited to the December 2013 graft probe. I also saw too many cases related to unsolved murders — hundreds in ten years! Even the Deniz Feneri charity organization was involved in a serious embezzlement scandal. But I also personally witnessed how the prosecutors oversaw the case related to Millî İstihbarat Teşkilatı (MIT) trucks that shipped weapons to groups in Syria. (The MIT was the national intelligence organization.) The prosecutors overseeing this case ended up in the stands of the accused as defendants, although they were innocent. I lamented the condition in which they found themselves.

By the time I had been a court reporter for a couple of years, I had become quite well known. And I had learned enough about the rule of law that I had become critical of how cases were being handled. In July 2016, I witnessed numerous people being arrested by the police, and I saw videos of them being tortured. I posted those pictures on my social media account.

"It is a crime against humanity!" I said in my posts. "You cannot torture anyone."

After that, the police tried to punish me by claiming that I was spreading the propaganda of a terrorist organisation. I just reminded them of the common rule of law all around the world.

Eventually, on July 17, 2016, I became the first journalist in Turkey to have their house raided by the police. While it is good to be on the top of the list, it's also a little stressful. ("What would you do with me in that turmoil, brother?" I asked myself in Turkish.)

Your past is everything you cannot give up. On my last day in Ankara, without leaving anything that I could not give up, I took the jacket I found at home and threw my life into the garbage. The rebellious girl had become a rebellious woman. People's ages and appearances can change, but their souls don't.

When the arrest warrant was issued for me in October, I realized I had to try to escape. Leaving the house where my parents and daughters were, I didn't even say goodbye so that it wouldn't be known how painful leaving was. I didn't want to give any goodbye hugs or say farewell — I didn't want my parents to be afraid of their daughter's leaving, and I didn't want my daughters to understand that their mother was leaving.

Before opening the door to exit, I turned and looked at my family for the last time. My father was watching us in shock; he had no idea what to do. He had no power to help me. My mother was always scared of everything, but she was a respectful person who always looked innocent. She and I were so different from each other; she never fought with anyone, unlike me who was never scared of anyone. Yet I think my mother and I were feeling the same pain as I departed, and I suspect she was wondering why her daughter was leaving her children. And we had this in common: my mother and I were both mothers who were losing their children.

My eight-month-old daughter was crawling on the carpet with her pacifier in her mouth. Her sister was sitting on the sofa because she did not understand what the separation would be. "Why do I have to leave?" I thought. "I am not a criminal!"

I pulled the door and went out quickly.

My daughters did not understand how the world can be unjust. My experiences, injustice, and my work had forced me to leave my baby and my girl. My past remains in my mind as a photo of a baby crawling on the carpet. I would not see them again for three and a half years.

When I escaped from my country, I was thirty-five years old, with thirty-five years of memories of childhood, family, and work. But when I left for Canada, it felt as if that one day was fixed in my mind as the one I would remember. Not the days before or the days after — just that one single day.

Geography was not destiny, but it was a garbage dump that took mothers from their babies and threw books into the garbage.

We were books whose covers were torn, whose titles and authors were feared.

We were rebels.

We were anarchists.

That is why crying was a shame, so I cried secretly to the nursing babies I left in the derelict dump. Nobody saw my tears, and nobody knew.

While I was leaving the country, there were still books that were being thrown away because being an educated writer was considered criminal.

Let's take a chance, I thought, and hit the road for freedom. For the next five months, I lived an underground life. It was a runaway's existence, but because I had grown up in crisis, always the "fighter woman," I had been trained for such moments. The road was long, and it continued with many stories on the way.

I came all the way to Canada.

When I arrived, I was crying for everything I had lost. Now I bemoan that, although I had fought for justice, there is no justice. I had sought the truth, but there is no truth. Everything I had lost and had believed in were lies.

Here, nights have passed again with books. I realized that I had not discovered just any book in that trash bin, but rather my life story, "The Sea of Sorrows."

Like a poem.

True to life and full of emotion, a story of a castaway and a refugee.

And I understand that I had never actually been a person of fighting and wrestling. There is a hunger and yearning in my soul for books and knowledge. Not for violence.

"Putting pen to paper lights more fire than matches ever will," said Malcolm S. Forbes.

I burned, I was burnt, and I escaped.

Even if your culture dictates that your fate is determined in advance, you can still find your essence. Geography does not have to be your whole destiny.

Your destiny can sometimes appear in the garbage.

I have had a lot of time to think in this calm, orderly, and quiet country.

You think that survival in a geography is based on violence and fighting. Authors write as if they are actually fighting (on paper); hatred flows from their language and from their knowledge.

Yet a poetry book had changed my life.

First, it was a journey to freedom; now I have found myself at the end of that road.

I was no longer the girl who had played soccer in the fields in Ufuktepe (in Ankara) and knocked the boys down. I had been that book thrown away in the trash, that book that had changed my life.

Alexander Duarte
(Venezuela)

ALEXANDER DUARTE is a Venezuelan journalist with degrees in Social Communications and in Politics and International Law. Alexander began working as a journalist in 1992 at *El Nacional*, one of the most important newspapers in Venezuela, as a press and then radio reporter, and then in 2001 became director of Media and Public Relations with the Attorney General of Venezuela. In 2019, as conditions for journalists in the country deteriorated and he found his life in danger, he escaped Venezuela with his family and they came to Canada as refugees.

Far from Venezuela: Stuck in Limbo

VENEZUELA IS LOCATED on the northern coast of South America. It is a nation with vast mineral resources, such as gold, iron, diamonds, and oil, and in the twentieth century became the fourth richest country on Earth by extracting these resources. This land, which saw the birth of Simón Bolívar, the liberator of five nations, is the place of such natural wonders as the Gran Sabana (The Great Savannah), the Pico Bolívar (Bolívar's Peak), Los Roques, and the Salto Ángel (Angel Falls). The latter is a waterfall with an uninterrupted plunge of 807 metres.

In short, many of us Venezuelans feel love and an indescribable sense of pride for the fatherland that gave light to those who, in the nineteenth century, defeated the Spanish Empire; the fatherland that became a symbol of democracy in Latin America from 1958 to 1998, only to see that democracy end when Hugo Chávez, a former soldier who six years prior had been imprisoned for attempting a coup, became president of the republic. Once in power, Chávez established a ruthless military regime and a criminal organization with international influence that even today, more than a decade after Chavez's death, plunders Venezuela's riches and tortures its people under the fake banner of a socialist ideology.

It would take hundreds of pages to explain how Venezuela became one of the poorest countries on Earth. But, at the same time, it would take even more pages to express the love I feel for my nation. I love Venezuela so much that, if reincarnation were real, my biggest wish would be to open my eyes once again in this paradise, to see its light once again.

Before I continue, I want to make one thing clear: I was not born to migrate, either by choice or by force. However, perhaps because of an

excess of arrogance or nationalistic pride, destiny had other plans. I had
to migrate by force.

Maybe I could explain the aforementioned arrogance, the assertion
that I was not born to migrate, by stating that, in the twentieth century,
my country became the preferred destination for many immigrants. We
received people from Spain, Portugal, Italy, Lebanon, China, Bolivia,
Colombia, Ecuador, and Chile. We even received a fair share of Germans
who, in 1843, had established a small settlement in a mountainous zone
sixty kilometres north of Caracas that came to be known as La Colonia
Tovar.

We don't always get what we desire. Life is made up of countless twists
and turns; it is a tornado that will take us to the places we least expect,
even if some cognitive theories posit that we can visualize and decree our
destiny. In my case, such things were not always successful.

For example, when I was a child, I never expected to be a journalist.
On the contrary, I wished to be an archaeologist, a pilot, an astronaut on
his way to the moon, or maybe travel to the centre of the Earth. But I never
dreamed of becoming a journalist. Nevertheless, ever since I learned how
to read, I was interested in books. I dreamed of being an adventurer while
I immersed myself in the stories of Robinson Crusoe, Gulliver, *Treasure
Island*, Tom Sawyer, and Hans Christian Andersen, among others. I also
used to read the Bible, not out of spiritual interest, but because I saw it as
a book full of fascinating adventures — one of the many my father had
acquired. I delighted myself reading about Samson and Delilah, Noah's
ark, the Jewish exodus from Egypt, and the story of Jesus being harassed
by the Devil in the desert.

After finishing high school, I began my studies at the School of Me-
chanical Engineering at the Universidad Central de Venezuela in Caracas.
There I became involved in a faculty magazine, in which I used to write
articles about politics. That was in 1988, when Venezuela was still a democracy, and we still had the privilege of expressing our ideas and views
without fear of persecution or censorship. A classmate, who confessed he
was an avid reader of my articles, suggested I study journalism. Due to his
energetic exhortation, I believe he might have been my Devil in the desert.

And it isn't that my friend was pushing me towards evil, but, in time, I learned that journalism is one of the most dangerous careers in the world. You receive flattery if you become a mouthpiece to those in power, but if you decide to tell the truth you might risk your freedom, even your life.

Back then, why would have I considered such risks? Let's say I became a victim of temptation and decided to abandon engineering and join the School of Communications. It was a five-year degree, and, after my graduation, I went to grad school and got a master's degree in international law and politics. And, before even graduating, I already had my first job as spell-checker and graphic designer in a newspaper focused on economics. During a national convention of journalism students in August 1993, I met my brave and beloved wife, an honest journalist with whom I have shared great pride in being members of our profession.

It is not possible for me to tell in detail the reasons why we fled our beloved country, as the regime that flogs our nation has eyes and ears all over the world. However, I can say that we fled after becoming whistleblowers, releasing information that hurt the dictatorship. I can also say we were tried in absentia for "betraying the Fatherland." For these reasons, I originally chose to write under the pseudonym Santiago de Leon as an ode to Caracas, my place of birth, which had been named Santiago de Leon de Caracas when it was founded in 1567. However, my desire to write under a pseudonym was conquered by a strong temptation to write under my real name. It took me a long time to make this choice, to convince myself, but I have never been one to fear the consequences of my journalistic temptations. And yet, I still cannot stop worrying about others, and I have tried not to release more information about the corruption in my country's justice system, as my family would be at risk of being kidnapped and tortured. This is the way in which the oppressive forces of the regime enforce silence on those like me, those who have managed to escape from their claws.

After getting married, my wife and I worked as reporters in various forms of media. In 1997, I was hired by one of the most important newspapers in Venezuela, *El Nacional*, where I became a member of the team in charge of covering politics. I was assigned to cover what today is known

Alexander Duarte

as the National Assembly, but back then was called the Congress of the Republic. Our democracy wasn't perfect, but it was tolerant. While covering Congress, I witnessed how members of opposing parties would angrily argue with each other during sessions, and then, once these sessions finished, would go out to eat lunch together or drink some coffee. It wasn't rare for journalists like me to join these politicians during lunch, always in search of news.

In 1998, a new electoral year began. Hugo Chávez, after being pardoned by the president for his attempted coup of February 4, 1992, decided to run for president. I was one of the first journalists to interview this new candidate. It was a Sunday morning and he had decided to meet with a small number of followers in Catia, a low-income area in Caracas. During his first few weeks as a candidate, Chávez could not boast of having many followers and supporters. However, once he made his idea of dissolving Congress public, polls began to favour him. His support grew, and, in December of 1998, he won the presidency of the republic.

His first orders as president fulfilled his two biggest campaign promises: to dissolve Congress and to convene the Constituent National Assembly to draft a new constitution. At the beginning of his administration, due to an accelerated growth of international oil prices, Venezuela experienced a new, but ephemeral, economic boom. The boom's ephemerality came about because the millions of dollars that the country made, which were supposed to be equally redistributed, ended up in the pockets of the military officers and civilians who made up the regime, leading the country's economy to deteriorate.

Despite putting all of their hope in Chávez, who every day promised to fight against poverty and turn Venezuela into an economic superpower, Venezuelans began to realize that the social crises of the past not only persisted but had worsened. Meanwhile, members of the regime, who had previously lived moderate lives, did not spare in boasting about their luxury cars, homes, and large bank accounts in foreign countries.

On April 11, 2002, after a multitudinous demonstration and the deaths of nineteen Venezuelans at the hands of armed men loyal to Chávez, the president was ousted and imprisoned by a group of soldiers. A transition government was immediately established once Chávez was in prison. However, three days later, another group of soldiers took Chávez out of prison and put him back in power. These events became an excuse for Chávez to radicalize his administration, beginning with the expropriation of corporations, the implementation of a currency exchange control, and the persecution of dissenters and members of the opposition. Of course, this persecution was expanded to include the media, and, as in every oppressive regime, journalists were targeted. In order to quell the growing discontent among the population, expressed through large protests, Chávez began to develop several social programs aimed at economic aid, known as *misiones* (missions). These *misiones* were supposed to offer aid to low-income families, unemployed mothers, destitute people, university students, and Indigenous people, among others.

Despite the development of social programs, the economic crisis got worse by the day. The *misiones* would only help a few, while those in charge of administering them made money, getting richer and richer through the embezzlement of funds. Meanwhile, Chávez blamed the crisis on the United States, which he believed was waging economic warfare against Venezuela. The threat only existed in his head, but Chávez used his anti-imperialist speeches to call on supporters to fight *"rodilla en tierra"* — "with their knee to the ground," an expression that was meant to symbolize loyalty to the regime. Everything that happened in Venezuela began to be blamed on foreign governments, and on supposed internal enemies. As a consequence, Chávez never admitted that the income from oil was being embezzled by his inner circle, including his siblings and children, who went from living humble lives to being millionaires.

However, Chávez's stealing the money that belonged to the people of Venezuela was not enough for Chávez's allies; they began to involve themselves in drug trafficking. It is no secret that the drug ring *Cartel de los Soles* (Cartel of the Suns) is led by high-ranking officers of the armed forces of Venezuela. Journalist Mauro Marcano spoke out about this organization and was assassinated on September 1, 2004; so too was Orel Zambrano, the head of the magazine ABC, on January 16, 2009. Since Chávez rose to power, twenty-two journalists have been murdered in Venezuela. To these murdered journalists, one must add the dozens of journalists injured by supporters of the regime, and the dozens of journalists who have been persecuted, imprisoned, and tortured by the police and the military. The regime has even detained and deported foreign reporters, destroying their equipment in the process.

In order to suppress his dissenters, Chávez shielded himself behind the police forces of the nation and the military. Moreover, he created the so-called Bolivarian Circles, militias formed by gangs coming out of low-income zones from around the country. These militias, in exchange for keeping political dissidents scared and under control, received money, drugs, and vehicles from the government.

Despite keeping his opposition in line, Chávez was not able to defeat an insurmountable enemy: death, which was attributed to colon cancer. Officially, the government claims Chávez died on March 5, 2013, in Caracas. However, there are many signs that he might have died in Cuba in December 2012. I had the opportunity to meet two of his most trusted bodyguards, one of whom accompanied Chávez to Cuba, and confirmed Chávez did not return to Caracas alive. Nevertheless, his most loyal supporters made the country believe, during the first two months of 2013, that their Supreme Commander was alive and that he signed documents, exercised, and received visits at the Military Hospital in Caracas. No member of the public can confirm this; no one ever saw him.

In December 2012 before leaving for Cuba, where he would receive treatment for his cancer, Chávez told his followers that, in case he were to die, they would have to support Nicolás Maduro. Maduro immediately began to work behind the scenes, negotiating with the military to support his claim to power. He knew that he needed to do so to counter Diosdado Cabello, one of the soldiers who had accompanied Chávez during his 1992 coup attempt and a person who held enormous influence over the military. When Maduro came to power, he gave members of the military political offices, such as ministries. Political offices were not enough, however; Maduro also gave members of the military control of companies in charge of clothing, construction, agriculture, banks, and media. He even gave them the power to negotiate oil rates with other countries. This information was confirmed by researchers at the Organized Crime and Corruption Reporting Project.

Months prior to Chávez's death, large lines to acquire food could be seen outside supermarkets. Hundreds of Venezuelans would stand in line for hours, sometimes overnight, in order to acquire rice, milk, coffee, and other basic necessities. However, standing in line did not guarantee that these products would reach people's hands.

The crisis grew day by day. Food production companies had not functioned properly since they were expropriated by Chávez and handed over to his closest allies. Many of these companies had to declare bankruptcy due to the lack of qualified personnel to keep them afloat, and due to funds destined for food production ending in bank accounts in foreign countries. In consequence, the regime created new import enterprises to bring in food from countries like Mexico, which, regardless of the quality of the food, sent boxes to Venezuela. These boxes were then distributed to those who held cards identifying them as members of the PSUV (United Socialist Party of Venezuela). In other words, in order to receive said food boxes, one needed to be a supporter of the regime. A similar situation developed in order to acquire medicines and medical supplies. In this way, the regime found a perfect way to inflate their number of followers, control the population, and manipulate electoral choices.

As a consequence of starvation due to food shortages, people around the country began searching in the trash outside of restaurants trying to find even the smallest bite to eat. Some of them would end up fighting over food with rats, cats, and dogs. Some of these animals ended up on the stoves of these starving people.

On April 14, 2013, just over a month after Chávez's death was announced, presidential elections were held. It is estimated that seventy-nine per cent of Venezuelans participated in the election. However, despite his lack of support, and with the National Electoral Council controlled by the regime, Maduro declared himself the winner over the opposition candidate, Henrique Capriles. Two years later, on December 6, 2015, Venezuela held parliamentary elections. This time, Venezuelans went to the polls in droves, giving the opposition control of the National Assembly. The opposition gained the ability, through its majority, to remove Maduro and call new elections.

Nevertheless, after losing control of the National Assembly, Maduro's regime began implementing a series of desperate measures in order to hinder the administration and performance of the new assembly deputies, who were to be sworn in on January 5, 2016. To ensure this happened, Maduro sought absolute control of the Supreme Court, which would help him block the activities of the assembly. He ordered that, before the new deputies were sworn in, the former deputies must confirm thirteen Supreme Court justices and twenty-one alternate justices, all of them allies and supporters of the regime. This order was achieved through the violation of the Constitution and the rule of law since Maduro's nominees did not meet the academic requirements to become justices. Moreover, several of these nominees were under investigation by the Attorney General for corruption. Some of the nominees had criminal records related to homicide, sexual assault, and other crimes and felonies. It is well known that Maikel Moreno, current president of the Supreme Court, was accused, tried, and sentenced in 1987 and 1989 for the murders of a woman and a man.

After the illegal swearing-in of the new justices, the Supreme Court, completely controlled by Maduro, began to issue orders by which it assumed legislative functions and withdrew immunity from the National Assembly deputies. On March 31, 2017, Luisa Ortega Díaz, who at the time was still the Attorney General and who was known as a loyal *chavista*, decided to publicly denounce the illegal judicial process and the violation of the Constitution. At the same time, Díaz made evidence widely available that proved the Supreme Court's illegitimacy.

Díaz was removed from office by the new Constituent National Assembly, which had been hastily created in an attempt to dissolve the legitimate National Assembly. Due to her removal from office, and the threat of being sent to prison, Luisa Ortega Díaz fled to Colombia with the help of a group of soldiers disenchanted with the regime. Since then, the fury of the regime has intensified, and it has increasingly targeted the journalists who spread Díaz's statements and evidence.

By then, my wife and I had managed to flee with our children to the United States. Weeks prior we had been alerted that the regime planned to arrest us, and to send us and many other journalists to La Tumba, an underground prison located in the basement of the Bolivarian National Intelligence Service (SEBIN) headquarters. Over the years, La Tumba has become one of the regime's favourite places to imprison journalists and dissidents, who are locked in small dark cells without ventilation. Prisoners are only allowed to exit their cells in order to be tortured; reports state that some prisoners are forced to eat their own waste. Others are never seen again. The case of political prisoner Fernando Albán comes to mind; Albán died while being tortured in 2018. His body was thrown from the top of the headquarters, and his death was ruled a suicide.

We managed to escape the country thanks to the previously mentioned bodyguards, who helped us evade airport security checks. One of my wife's brothers, who was already living in Canada, told us that here we would be able to seek asylum, and he would wait for us on the border between Buffalo and Fort Erie.

As soon as we were able, we travelled to Buffalo where we received help from Vive la Casa, an organization that shelters refugees from all around the world and helps them enter Canada. We spent a month in one of Vive's shelters, until we were notified that we had been summoned for an appointment at the border. After a long day of filling forms and interviews, we were welcomed to Canada and given a date for our refuge hearing.

We had stopped being scared, but I must admit I felt uncomfortable having to sign a document in which we accepted being deported if we were not granted refugee status in Canada. By the date of the hearing, April 28, 2017, Venezuela had ceased to be a safe place for us, a safe place for journalists. Being deported from Canada would mean going back to a place where we would be imprisoned, tortured, and maybe murdered.

I feel I must add that, in 2019, the United Nations High Commissioner for Human Rights, and Chile's former president, Michelle Bachelet had denounced the 7,000 extrajudicial executions that had been carried out in Venezuela, and the more than 350 members of the Venezuelan opposition who remained in prison in terrible conditions.

We arrived in Toronto, Canada, with barely $250. We still had a few possessions, like our wedding rings, but we felt we needed to sell them in order to buy food and pay for a room to stay in. I took our wedding rings to a jewellery store in downtown Toronto, where I was offered three hundred dollars for both of them, even though they were worth more. After getting the money, I left the store, sat down on a bench, and began crying.

A few months after coming to Toronto, a Colombian friend we had made took us to Romero House. Without any complications, we were offered a place to stay in for a year with our three children.

Nevertheless, the fear of being deported remained. However, it slowly went away once Canada had granted us refugee status. My children and wife cried tears of happiness. We had all gone through a year full of uncertainties since we'd left our country. We had lived with the hope of one day going back, but every day that dream became ever more distant. Nevertheless, we were refugees now, but they felt safe, and they felt sheltered from the dangers that had threatened us.

I hugged them and shared their happiness, but I was torn inside. I had hoped that the Attorney General's statements and the international backlash towards the regime would lead to its end, and my country would return to democracy and freedom. This never happened, and things just got worse as time went on. In September of 2022, the United Nations confirmed that the number of Venezuelans who have fled the regime is now more than 6.8 million, surpassing Syria as the country with the most people who have left their homes and become refugees.

To leave my country, without intention to do so, has made me understand the suffering of thousands of people around the world who have been displaced by wars and famine. Even today, even when I enjoy the safety the Canadian government provides me, I feel like a prisoner of a dictatorship that stops me from returning to my country. I am the prisoner of a dictatorship that stopped me from seeing my father before his death, in April of 2018, after suffering several seizures due to the lack of medicine. I am the prisoner of a dictatorship that stopped me from seeing my mother before she died in August of 2019, due to pulmonary complications. We are prisoners of a dictatorship that did not allow my wife to be next to her suffering mother before she died in December 2020, due to COVID-19.

Today, I feel stuck in limbo because, as I said, I was not born to migrate. I was born to enjoy life to the fullest in my own land, to taste the flavours of our food, to rest on the sand of our warm beaches, to be under our sun and our clear skies, to listen to our music, to enjoy the laughter of our people, and to hug my siblings.

As an immigrant, as a refugee, I have been struggling with writer's block. My mind wanders off to think about those who suffer in Venezuela, to think about our families and whether they have food on their tables. We have faced the barriers that come with not being fluent in a new language. However, every day I thank God that we had the opportunity to give our children the best education we were able to, that they began learning to speak English after learning how to say their first words in Spanish. But it has been hard for my wife and me, after so many years studying as undergrads and grads in Venezuela, after working for years as journalists, to find ourselves working as we do: one as cleaner in a long-term care facility, the other as an Uber driver.

Yet, we have jobs and the ability to provide for our children. We have, moreover, the pride of not having succumbed to the temptation of taking the money we were offered to stay silent. Today we can look our children in the eye without being ashamed of anything we've done, and with the knowledge that we have been honest. I can look my children in the eye knowing that we had the courage to refuse to collaborate with a dictatorship that has forced millions of Venezuelans to flee, who, I am sure, were also not born to migrate and now suffer xenophobic attacks at the hands of people in countries we always welcomed in Venezuela.

Today, our mutual consolation is knowing that our parents, who were aware of the dangers we were under, never shed a tear in our presence when we told them we had to flee Venezuela. We can console ourselves with the knowledge that our parents were unconditionally supportive and proud of us, and they remain our inspiration to keep standing up for what we believe in, and our inspiration to keep moving forward ... even if we never got to see them again. I emphasize: I was not born to migrate, but I do not regret having made that choice. I did not want to be a journalist either, but it was the best choice I have ever made.

Maria Saba
(Iran)

An Ottawa-based writer, storyteller, and arts educator, **MARIA SABA** was born and raised in Iran. Writing in both English and Farsi, she has published three books and over a hundred articles, interviews, and stories in four continents. Maria's short story manuscript, "My First Friend," was a semi-finalist for the Iowa Short Fiction Prize, and the title story, published in *Scoundrel Time*, won the Editor's Choice Award and was nominated for the Pushcart Prize. Her novella *The Secret of Names* was longlisted for the 2020 Disquiet Literary Prize. Maria has served on various arts and literature juries and is the recipient of grants in English literature from Canada Council for the Arts, the Ontario Arts Council, Saskatchewan Arts Board, and the City of Ottawa. She attended Bread Loaf Writers Conference, Banff Writing Studio and residencies at Banff, the Al Purdy A-Frame in Ameliasburgh, and the Tyrone Guthrie Centre in Ireland. She recently won the PEN Canada Scholarship and the Wallace Stegner Grant for the arts. Currently Maria is working on her novel, *There You Are.*

"Walls have mice, mice have ears" is the phrase I remember most from my childhood in Iran. If this doesn't instill the fear of "talking" in a child, I don't know what will. I remember sitting by myself imagining mice running in walls, carrying messages to someone out there, waiting to hear what we said.

The "mice in the walls" were nothing compared to what happened after the 1979 revolution: execution, stoning, and an all-encompassing invasion of personal life.

The tremendous need to record and recount these experiences inspired me to re-enact them in works of literature. "Lenovichi," the opening chapter to my novel, is a reflection on growing up under a dictatorship. The story comments on the vulnerability and the innate need of a child for a sense of trust and friendship amidst the harsh, brutal world of the grown-ups.

Lenovichi

"HELLO." THE KIND, gentle voice of a man came from behind the apartment door. Inside, Manisa held her breath and didn't say anything.

"Hello," the voice repeated.

"Hello," Manisa said to be polite, then regretted it immediately.

"I am a friend of your parents."

Her hand went to her mouth, but she stopped herself. "They're not in," she said, pressing her lips together. Staring at the jagged nails, she forgot about the voice. If she didn't chew her nails for a week, she would get a new set of crayons. Forty-eight colours. Mommy had promised. Tomorrow would be a week. Or was it the day after. She heard a cough and remembered the stranger. "I can't open the door to strangers."

"You are very wise," the voice said, genially. "But your parents asked me to stay with you. And a promise is a promise."

"They wanted to take comrade hatter's dad to the hospital," Manisa giggled. "His name is comrade Kaveh. Daddy says I shouldn't call him 'hatter.' But he never takes off his hat. Not even in the summer. Not in the apartment. Never ever."

The man chuckled a little too but said nothing.

"He is not in Tehran. His daddy is sick. Very sick. So, Mommy and Daddy had to go. Granddad will pick me up. We're all going to be at Granddad's."

"Tell you what. I'll just sit here and keep busy until your grandpa gets here. I don't care how long it takes."

Manisa hesitated before asking. "What will you do?"

"Um. Not much to do out here. There is no chair or anything, but don't you worry. Just let me make myself comfortable."

"How?" she asked and considered pulling an armchair from under the window to the door for him, but she had to open the door first.

"I am spreading my handkerchief on the ground," the man said. "Here, I am sitting, nice and comfortable. Mind you, the tiles are quite cold, but don't you worry about me."

Manisa pressed her ear to the door, but there was no sound. She slid down and sat on the floor. "What are you doing?" she finally asked.

"Well … to tell you the truth, it's a secret. Are you good at keeping secrets?"

"I am, I am," she nearly shouted. "My drawing of Daddy. It's a secret. I was just signing it. Granddad taught me to draw. He wants to teach me to paint too. He says, everyone says, I am good at it." She paused, and her breath came out in a whoosh.

"I bet you are," the voice said without hesitation. "I bet you're good at so many things. If only I could see your drawing. I wish my daughter would do that for me, but bless her little heart, she has no such talent."

Manisa half rose. "Is she with you?"

"No. She is home with her mother," the man said. "It must be hard to be all by yourself," he continued. "My daughter is so afraid of being alone."

"I'm not afraid," Manisa claimed, and squatted down.

"Of course, *you* are not," he said with such confidence that he convinced Manisa she was not afraid. "But my daughter is. She is very clever and sweet. You sound so much like her. Would you like to see her?"

"Now?!"

"No, not now. It will take a long time to go home and bring her. What do I tell your parents if I left you alone?"

"Next time?" she said with a sigh, unable to hide her disappointment. He promised to bring her next time.

"So, tell me," he said. "This drawing of yours, why is it a secret?"

"It's for Daddy's birthday? Didn't he tell you it's his birthday?"

The man paused. "No, I don't believe he did. Mind you he was in a rush. Wait a second. Let me just stretch my legs here. So, this is your surprise for him. What a great idea! Did you just draw it today?"

"Oh, no. Days and days."

"And he, your father, knows nothing about it?"

"No," she cried out. "No one, nobody knows."

"Ouch! But if you shout like that, everyone will know," the man said with a chuckle.

"You must be really good at hiding things. Maybe you can help me."

The voice felt closer now. "Help *you*? How?" She pressed her ear to the door, lest she missed a word.

"You see, I want to give my daughter a present —"

"What? Crayons? A doll? Is it her birthday?"

"No. It's next week. I haven't decided what to get her yet. But just like you, I want it to be a surprise. If only I had an idea where to hide it. Do you ever find the things your parents hide from you?"

"They do all the time. But they think I don't know," Manisa bragged. "Mostly at nights when they think I am asleep. Daddy hides things in the secret cabinet behind my poster. The photo of me. How clever of Daddy. He made it into a poster. A secret cabinet is under the poster!"

"Amazing! Your dad is very smart for sure," the voice said.

"There's the cooler pipes on the roof," she said.

"You mean ... the cooler ducts? Oh my, oh my! That's very clever."

"Not my presents. Just papers, books, once a typewriter." Her hand went to her mouth, and she suddenly stopped. "You won't tell anyone?" she said, in a mere whisper.

"And why would I do that?" he sounded a bit hurt. "If I tell my daughter, how can I hide anything from her? Besides, I love secrets and surprises. Don't you?"

Manisa hesitated, her fingers dug into her palms. The secret had been bubbling inside her for days. Now that it was out, the tingling in her tummy — she was sure that was where secrets were kept — was gone.

"I bet your father will be so happy," he said, with a sigh.

"I can draw you," Manisa said, in a conciliatory tone.

"Really? Do you mean it? No one has ever drawn me."

She had suggested to draw him and yet hadn't even opened the door to … what was his name? Did he say? She couldn't remember. She peeled herself from the door and faced it. "What is your name?"

There was a pause. "Um … my name … is Mr. Ahmadi," he said. Mr. Ahmadi sounded like a serious grown-up name, like friends of Granddad and Grandma.

"I wish I could properly introduce myself, but no matter. I am very excited about your drawing me. Will you do that? Really? But how?"

Manisa sprang up and turned the key. The door opened.

A big man with a goatee, standing tall and straight, held out his hand. "Hello again. I am Mr. Ahmadi. And you are —"

"Manisa." Still standing in the doorway, she extended her hand. Unlike other grownups, who mimicked a handshake or worse, patted her on the head, he shook her hand firmly.

She drew back, and he entered.

Her eyes followed him moving towards her father's armchair. Mr. Ahmadi was taller than him but much bigger. He was not old, like her granddad. But he was not young, like her daddy. What was he then?

"May I?" he asked.

She nodded and hesitated before sitting down in the other armchair, and when she did, she kept shifting on her seat uneasily. There was something unsettling about Mr. Ahmadi's broad shoulders covering the whole back of the chair. His elbows pushed against the arms of the chair as if to make more room. Her daddy fell into the chair, leaving room for her to sit on one arm and extend her legs to the other. She squirmed and her index finger got caught in a ripped seam of the cushion.

Mr. Ahmadi smiled again. He had a nice, large dimple on his cheek, like her daddy. "Can I bother you for a glass of water?" He leaned forward and gently touched her arm.

"Yes." Slowly she pulled her finger out. "There is tea, too."

"Why not? Let's have tea."

He followed her into the kitchen and watcher her climb on the stool. Before she reached for the kettle, he grabbed it. "Let me," he said. She pointed to an upper cabinet. "Glasses are there."

"You know what, water is fine." He picked a glass from the cabinet Manisa had pointed to and filled it with water.

"So, tell me, will you really do a portrait of me?"

She nodded, smiling. Her legs extended under the table; her knees locked.

"But first ..." He pointed to the notebook in front of her on the table. On the cover, there was a large elephant lifting a brush. "Do I get to see the ..." He asked, his index finger on the tip of his nose.

"Yes. Let me sign it first." She opened the notebook and scribbled on the bottom right of a black and white drawing before sliding it across the table.

"Goodness." He raised his thick eyebrows and blinked twice, as if he couldn't believe his eyes. "*You* drew *this*?"

The sparkle in his eyes reminded her of her grandfather's whenever he looked at her drawings. Her knees unlocked; her legs dangled carefree.

"You remind me so much of my daughter," he said, fixing his gaze on her. "She's clever, almost as pretty as you."

Her cheeks felt warm. He thought she was pretty. "Does your daughter swim?"

"Oh, no," he said, with a mild laugh. "Guess what else she's afraid of?"

Manisa considered this for a moment. "Water!" They both said it at the same time and burst into laughter.

"That's right," he said, as he slapped his hand on the table. "One day I should bring her by. I bet you're a good swimmer. Maybe you can teach her how to swim. Will you do that?"

"Um ... We don't have a pool," she said. "Granddad does."

"Well, maybe your grandfather doesn't mind my bringing her by some time."

"Yes. And Daddy or Mommy can teach her. They're champions. At the university."

"Yes, of course," he said, with an admiring look. "I remember your father from the university days: '71 or '72 maybe, but it feels like ages ago. Your father was excellent in everything he did. Your mom, too. Both so attractive."

"Granddad always says the same. Grandma too," she said.

"So, this is going to be a surprise, you said?"

"Yes. Until tonight," she said calmly, trying to conceal her excitement. She didn't want to sound childish.

He blinked a few times as if the sun was in his eyes, or maybe it was a twitch. He turned away from her. "You are such a thoughtful daughter," he nearly whispered.

"What is her name?"

"Huh?" He turned to her, agape.

"Your daughter."

"Oh ... um ... her name is Mitra." He was frowning, not as in angry, but surprised. "This isn't your name." He pointed to the drawing in his hands.

She giggled and covered her mouth with her hand. "My drawing name."

"You mean you actually have an artistic name?" When she nodded, he continued. "And what name is that?"

"The first time Daddy saw one of my drawings, he told Mommy that there was going to be another," she paused. "Leo ... nar ... do ... da ... Vin ... ci. But I said Lenovichi. Mommy said I should sign my drawings like that."

"Very becoming, your artistic name. I can't think of a better one."

He turned the page back and pointed to the man in the checkered shirt in the previous drawing. "I can imagine him sitting right here, exactly the way you drew."

"No, he wasn't here. He was at Grandma's," she explained. "In the basement. They can't play music here. The neighbours complain about the noise."

"I see," he said with interest, flipping through pages of drawings of Mommy and Daddy's friends. Then he closed the notebook.

"They must be proud of you," he said. "You have certainly captured their likenesses."

She smiled. She didn't know what "captured their likenesses" meant, but the way he said it made it sound like a good thing.

He leaned forward and lowered his voice as in the way of sharing a secret. "Now I want to tell you something."

She sat up, her gaze fixed on him.

"I am thinking …" He tugged at his beard, "… maybe we can surprise your parents."

She drew nearer, leaning forward, all attention. "How?"

"If we keep my coming here a secret, then I can surprise them. You see, we haven't seen much of each other for a long time. After the university days. So, it would be a big surprise for everyone to see me at your father's birthday. How about that?"

Manisa stared at him, mouth half-open. "You didn't see Daddy today?"

"Of course, I saw him today, but not properly. You know, to see everyone and the family and my family. To see my daughter. That would be a surprise."

"Like you were surprised to see me?" Manisa felt clever for figuring that out.

He nodded, and then he tilted his head, as if he had suddenly remembered something.

"It's here, right?" he asked.

"What?"

"The birthday."

She shook her head. "At Granddad's. Their house is huge. So, you'll bring Mitra too?"

His lips curled and uncurled. "Of course … that would be two surprises."

"Three!" she nearly shouted and finger counted. "My drawing, you, and Mitra. Three."

He smiled and nodded. "Maybe I should leave now. And then see you at the birthday."

She hesitated before sliding off the chair.

"Wait," she said. He waited for her patiently, not shifting like her parents did in the morning. She didn't want him to leave, but she couldn't think of anything to say. "Nothing."

"Okay then. So, when your parents come, no words." He touched the tip of his nose with his index finger. Manisa did the same with a big, conspiratorial smile.

In the hall, he extended his arm for another handshake. "Don't forget to lock the door," he said and waved good-bye.

Manisa stayed by the door long after his footsteps trailed off. Then she locked the door and hopped back to the kitchen. She took Mr. Ahmadi's glass — he didn't drink the water — and climbed on the stool, emptied the glass, and placed it on the plastic dish rack. She took her notebook into the hall and sat on the armchair. Closing her eyes, she let the scene of the surprise play in her head over and over, smiling all the time.

Manisa slipped out of the house into the garden and sat on the edge of the pool. Music carried from the living room where comrade Farid played guitar, and everyone sang in a language she didn't understand. She couldn't sit still. Her fingertips tingled, her tummy too. She extended her legs and retracted them. Again. And again, but the giddiness stuck to her. The thought of Mr. Ahmadi and Mitra showing up any minute made her want to jump up and down. She shook off her shiny, green sandals, drawing circles with her pointed toes on the tiles. What if they were lost? He didn't write down the address. What if they had knocked, but with all the noise, no one had heard? Barefoot, she headed for the gate and on tiptoe, lifted the latch and pulled it open a crack.

She thought she heard a voice from outside and ran back. Squatting behind a cypress, she watched the gate squeak and a man's head stuck in. Manisa half rose and sat back.

It was not Mr. Ahmadi. The man's head disappeared.

The gate opened further, enough for the man to slink in, then another man, and another. They scanned the garden, and some of them positioned themselves behind the cedars lining the path.

Maybe this is a surprise too. Maybe Mr. Ahmadi invited them. But nobody smiles. Where are the presents?

A short, stubby one in a dark suit nearly tripped over her sandal by the pool, but steadied himself and kicked it out of the way, cursing under his breath. Her hand flew to her mouth and her teeth dug in the edges of newly grown nails.

More men were coming. What did they want? They sure were up to something. A surprise!

Bilal Sarwary
(Afghanistan)

BILAL SARWARY is an Afghan journalist who has worked extensively with Western media outlets over the last twenty years in Afghanistan including the BBC for fourteen years. He is an independent scholar majoring in central linkages between warfare, drugs, and terrorism, and the FARC-ification of the Taliban. Bilal graduated in 2010 from Middlebury College in Vermont. Bilal was evacuated in August 2021 after the Taliban took over Afghanistan. He lives with his family in Toronto. Bilal is fluent in Pashto, Dari, Urdu, and English.

A Fatal Affair

May 1, 2023

A young Afghan journalist recounts the tragedy that unfolded as Taliban swept Afghanistan.

Listen to the reed and the tale it tells
How it sings of separation …
— Jalal-ud-Din Balkhi "Rumi" (1207–1273 CE/Sufi mystic/Balkh, Afghanistan)

OFTEN REFERRED TO as the Graveyard of Empires, Afghanistan became a republic in 1973 when Prime Minister Daud Khan deposed King Zaheer Shah and became the president. Communist as well as Islamist parties became more active during this period, which led to civil war, eventually culminating in the Soviet invasion of 1979.

The Soviets put up a puppet regime in Afghanistan, which worsened the civil strife. In 1986, the Soviet Red Army was forced to retreat in the face of heavy casualties inflicted by the very determined Mujahideen fighters. But disagreements between Mujahideen warlords and their failure to provide a stable government led to the rise of the Taliban, which seized Kabul in 1996 and imposed a brutal government based on strict interpretation of Islamic law.

The next five years — a black spot on the country's history — were marked by suppression of the people, widespread rights abuses, restrictions particularly aimed at women, and neglect of basic human values.

The regime fell following a U.S.-led invasion in 2001. Though toppled and pushed out of Kabul, the Taliban continued to wage an insurgency against U.S.-backed governments. It also continued to regroup and rearm, culminating in its return to power twenty years later.

The Rumble and the Tumble

We all knew Kabul would fall. But no one anticipated so soon.

It was just before eight on that sunny Sunday morning of August 15 when Brigadier General Mahmood Noorzai stepped into the Command Control Centre of Directorate 097. As head of the strike force, the dashing 6'2" general was responsible for eliminating all targets that posed a threat to Kabul.

All of thirty-six, Noorzai had a meteoric rise in the Afghan security forces. He started as a policeman in Helmand, rising through the ranks to become the province's counterterrorism director, then deputy police chief before joining the Afghan intelligence agency's special forces. Just days before, President Ashraf Ghani had named him chief of Afghanistan's counterterrorism department. Noorzai had been supposed to take charge of his new assignment in four days when a brisk sweep of destiny changed the course of his life.

"Over the past few days, rapid changes on the battlefield had kept us busy. Province after province was crumbling. The situation was evolving very fast," he said. "But our number one priority was Kabul."

"We had every single air asset — fighter jets, AC130 gunships, armed as well as surveillance drones — over Kabul. On the ground, two thousand Special Forces, one hundred armoured pickup trucks, dozens of Humvees, and twenty-five million rounds of ammunition were under my direct command, ready to be deployed within minutes."

On that Sunday morning, the Afghan forces seemed determined to defend their capital.

But then everything changed.

Around nine a.m., Noorzai received an SOS from a senior commander of the U.S. task force. Maidan Shahr — capital of Wardak province on the western edge of Kabul — was under attack. "Immediate reinforcements were needed."

There was no warning. No intelligence input. All of a sudden, the front line had shifted, and no one seemed to know.

Noorzai dispatched a special forces convoy to the besieged city. But by the time the soldiers arrived, Maidan Shahr had fallen. Afghan troops and policemen, who were entrusted to protect the city and its people, had fled their posts, giving Taliban a walkover.

This was the twenty-seventh provincial capital to fall.

Kabul was now just a couple of kilometres away.

More disappointing news came soon after.

Taliban had broken into Pul-e-Charkhi — the country's largest prison — on the eastern outskirts of Kabul, freeing hundreds of its fighters, Islamic State (Daesh) insurgents, and drug peddlers.

The Taliban was now at Kabul's doorstep.

By eleven a.m., chaos and confusion reigned on Kabul streets. Government officials and their families from the provinces were driving into the city to escape Taliban retribution. While the poor from the countryside who had taken refuge in Kabul to avoid the bloodshed were now rushing back. All roads leading in and out of Kabul were choked. Shops, offices, and businesses were shut. Criminals were looting whatever they could lay their hands on. There were no police in sight.

Even the men under Noorzai's command — who had till then been steadfast — were now losing their nerve.

"I got a call that men in my own command were fleeing their posts. These reports — sadly — turned out to be true."

Noorzai made frantic calls to his seniors, but no one answered. He then drove a truck to the army headquarters, only to find it deserted. He desperately tried to reach Ahmad Zia Saraj, interim director of National Directorate of Security — the Afghan intelligence agency — but didn't succeed. An SOS to army chief Lieutenant General Hebatullah Alizai's radio operator was not acknowledged. He was then told that President Ashraf

Ghani had fled the country.

Let down by his very "own," a dejected Noorzai reached the "safe house" that he often used for his work. He sat down on the steps, lit a cigarette, and broke down in tears.

It was six thirty p.m. The sun had set over Kabul.

(Gen Noorzai was evacuated from Kabul on the night of August 15. He is now in Australia with his wife, two daughters, and a son.)

The Bloody Pomegranates

The Kabul debacle was scripted long before in Afghanistan's dusty hinterland.

For months, the Taliban had been prodding Afghan security forces in the provinces, draining their energy and breaking their resolve, bit by bit.

But away from the eye, there was something else.

War fatigue was corroding the Afghan forces and the Afghan people from within.

"This war has destroyed generations," said Sayed Ahmad Jan, a police officer in Arghandab, a district in the southern province of Kandahar known for its pomegranates.

For Jan, this war was too personal.

The fifty-four-year-old said his two brothers — both policemen — were shot dead in front of him right on the doorstep of their family home.

Killing of government officials, policemen, and tribal elders had become a daily reality, he said.

"We are sick of this fighting. What has it given us? Nothing," said Jan. "I'm now the only breadwinner in a house which is full of widows and orphans."

As Jan sat down to have tea in his modest home, his police radio flashed one piece of distressing news after another from across the district.

"There's a whole generation of Afghans who have never seen peace. They have known life only from the shadows of guns and violence. They are tired of this uncertainty."

A deputy soon informed Jan that a Taliban fighter had driven an explosive-laden vehicle into a police post, killing thirteen policemen and himself in the suicide attack.

Many of those killed were personally known to Jan.

"Every day I attend the funeral of a dear one, say goodbye to a beloved friend," Jan said, getting into an unmarked police car. "Every day I pick up the pieces and start all over again.

"How long can one carry on like this?"

Jan said he mostly travels in a civilian car to outwit Taliban ambush teams lying in wait for officers like him.

"Our team has engaged insurgents in the pomegranate orchard there," an Afghan Special Forces commander, just known as Sharif, said, pointing to a green oasis a few metres away.

Before Jan could step out of his Toyota Corolla, a bullet grazed past his ear, leaving him bleeding and forcing everyone to duck for cover.

A Taliban sniper had taken the shot. Jan signalled his men to take positions and the whole place erupted in heavy machine gun fire. Jan was escorted to safety by Sharif.

"We keep losing our friends like this," said the young officer, looking in the direction of the gunfire. "There is so much pressure on the men. No one in my unit has taken a break in six months. I haven't had a shower in weeks. Just look at my beard," he said, pointing to his scruffy facial hair.

Jan's men, however, were lucky this time. There were fewer casualties among them. But the pomegranate garden was littered with the corpses of Taliban fighters.

"We are in a vicious cycle of violence, bloodshed, and heartbreak," Jan said, taking stock of the destruction. "Whether we kill them or they kill us, ultimately it's Afghanistan that bleeds."

(The Taliban claimed the capital of Kandahar on August 12, 2021. This was the eleventh provincial capital to fall within a week.)

The Tumult

Being known has its own pitfalls. I realized this when I fell into one.

The unfolding crisis had completely wrapped me up as a journalist. Stationed in my office in central Kabul's affluent Qala-e-Fathullah area, I was immersed in doing live interviews and two-ways for global news broadcasters who were ever so eager to know the minutest of details of the Taliban advance.

Qala-e-Fathullah was a quiet, tight-knit, friendly neighbourhood where everyone knew each other, where all looked out for one another. Neighbours would often call to check on your well-being, more so in these tumultuous times.

Shah was one such soft-spoken gentleman, living alone next door. He had been "missing" for the past few days, though, with just a huge padlock on his door greeting an occasional visitor instead of his wide grin.

It was about five a.m. on August 16. I had just concluded some of my live interviews when Ahmad, the security guard at my office, walked in.

"Shah *sahib* is here. Wants to see you," he whispered in my ear.

Elated at this unexpected arrival, I asked Ahmad, "What are you waiting for? Usher him in."

"Sir, it is better that you come out." Confused a bit by Ahmad's reply, I stepped out of the room.

A tall man with a short beard, Shah was standing there, stiff, with an AK-47 assault rifle looped over his shoulder.

"The Taliban wants you to know that you are safe," he announced as I tried to come to grips with the harsh reality.

Shah — I'm not sure if that was his real name — had been a Taliban intelligence operative all these years, and no one had the faintest idea.

About a year before, at dawn, Afghanistan's intelligence agency, the National Directorate of Security (NDS), had raided his home. The government had suspected him of working undercover for the Taliban.

The neighbours had then rubbished this charge and collectively petitioned the NDS to free him. Knowing well that I was in regular touch with top officials in the government, they had asked me to use my connections to secure his release.

Shah was released but only after I vouched for his high moral integrity.

"I'm here to return the favour," Shah said as he handed me a piece of paper with a mobile number scribbled on it. "If anyone in the name of Taliban comes to your door, call me."

"Someone just did!" I wanted to scream.

I was a known figure in Afghanistan. Born in the conflict, I had lived and survived, and risen from the very same conflict to earn a name for myself as a journalist. But in this emerging new order, that was turning out to be a problem.

Stunned by the early morning episode, I wobbled onto the street to buy some bread. Although my home was just ten metres from the office, I had not been home in the past week, eating and sleeping on the office floor whenever I could in between my live streams.

My wife, Fawzia, would call every now and then and assure me that she was fine, that my little daughter, Sola, was doing well although she missed her daddy.

The streets of Kabul, notoriously famous for their chaotic traffic, were largely empty. Most shops were shut. Distant gunfire, off and on, shattered the calm.

Somehow that usually short walk from my office to Mohammad Rasool's bakery on the main street seemed like an endless journey. Fear can have crippling consequences.

The bakery offered a delightful menu. But more than that, it was the charm Rasool served so lovingly that drew me to his bakery. Suave and soft-spoken, Rasool had come all the way from Badakhshan province to make Kabul his home.

Over the years, it had become my routine to stop by the bakery every morning and have a cup of green tea with bread while Rasool refreshed me with news of the neighbourhood. But that morning he seemed way out of his element.

"They have been asking about you," he murmured as soon as he saw me, lowering his head.

I felt a lump in my throat.

Being a visible anti-war face on global TV, it was not very difficult for the Taliban to locate me.

"Go away. Leave Kabul. Leave Afghanistan," Rasool said with a tear in his eye as he hurriedly handed me a loaf of bread and a can of Red Bull.

I couldn't figure out who was more in need of consolation — him or me.

Not even halfway to my office, I was accosted by two young, bearded men with long, flowing hair. Both had assault rifles hung on their shoulders. They needed no introduction.

Neither did I, I soon found out.

"I have seen you on TV," said the one with an AK-47 decorated with plastic flowers.

Shafiq Ahmad was his name, I later learned. This was his first visit to Kabul. In his early twenties, Ahmad was innocent to the extent of being downright naive. "Taliban has posted us here to keep an eye on you," he said, ignoring his colleague's gentle prod.

For now, the Red Bull bought some peace.

(Ahmad, the security guard, has moved back to his home province, Nangarhar. Shah *sahib* remains elusive. Mohammad Rasool still runs the bakery, but far away from Kabul.)

The Tipping Point

It was a rude awakening — literally and metaphorically.

Anxious and tired, I don't remember when I fell asleep on the office floor.

Ahmad, who had by now graduated from being just a security guard to a steno-typist-secretary, was sleeping in the small pantry next to the office area.

It was three in the morning when loud, violent bangs on the office door startled us out of slumber.

Through the peephole, we saw four armed Taliban soldiers. One of them was also carrying a military radio.

Seeing no response was forthcoming, the soldiers got angry and the beating on the door became even more agitated.

"Open up, Sarwary. We know you are in there," one of them shouted.

This was not a random security check. Nor was it a case of mistaken identity. This was a targeted attack.

Ahmad was scared and confused, but dead set to not let them in.

I gathered some courage and shouted back. "Taliban has given strict order to its fighters not to enter civilian homes. You are disobeying that order," I told them. "If you want, you can break the door, but I will not open it."

That seemed to have some calming effect. The pounding stopped. After a few minutes, they left. But as they walked away, one of them shouted, "We will be back."

This is not how I would have liked to begin my day. But in dark times, there is hardly any difference between night and day.

With most shops shut and supply chains disrupted, it was getting difficult to source even daily necessities. Prices had skyrocketed and shopkeepers were insisting on cash. But cash itself was scarce. There were long queues at ATMs and most banks had unofficially imposed a limit on withdrawals.

Towards the afternoon, I walked up to the Afghanistan International Bank in the neighbouring Shahr-e-Naw area, with whom I had enjoyed very cordial ties for more than a decade. One of the best banks in Afghanistan, I had entrusted it with all my life's savings.

A huge crowd had formed right at the entrance. The ATMs had run out of cash.

I somehow weaved my way through to reach the gate. The bank guard, a man in his thirties whom I had known for years, quickly let me in before shutting the gate behind my back.

"Sarwary *sahib*!" the manager's familiar voice greeted me.

A small stubby man with glasses, the manager was today carrying a different air of authority and wearing a belt holster with a handgun.

"You cannot withdraw any money," he said in an unusual, not-so-friendly tone.

The manager had been, it was soon revealed to me, a covert Taliban operative all along. He said, with pride, that he was recruited by the Taliban way back when he was a university student.

He had been biding his time and secretly passing on information on account holders who were considered "hostile" by the Taliban. I was one of them.

Broke — in every sense of the word — I wanted to cry my heart out.

(Prices of essential items have somewhat stabilised, but banks in Kabul still don't have cash. Taliban patrols are even now carrying out house-to-house searches, but the regime says they are part of a "clearing operation.")

Rock Bottom

As I gathered my pieces, my thoughts raced to my daughter, Sola, and my wife, Fawzia.

The Taliban were going to get me. And they wouldn't stop at that. For a moment, I couldn't breathe.

I needed to buy some time. I reached out to an old schoolmate who was now a top Taliban commander and a close ally of the new defence minister, Mullah Yaqoob, who was the son of Taliban founder Mullah Omar.

I had seen him since our school days — we'd met at the wedding of a common friend in my home province of Kunar. The young Talib's thick beard and wide-rim glasses covered almost his entire face. His eyes, barely visible, sparkled on seeing me after such a long time, but he spoke little and was mostly brusque with others. He did, though, give me his mobile number as I was leaving.

Now, he was a rising star in the Taliban ... and my only hope!

The schoolmate was quick to acknowledge the bind I was in. He spoke simultaneously about my situation with someone he was with and, after a few brief pauses, said, "Everything's going to be fine."

As he hung up, Ahmad called. Another Taliban squad had been to the office looking for me.

I could feel a panic attack coming.

I asked Ahmad to lock the office and disappear.

In my free time, I had compiled an "sos List" with names of people I knew would be there for me. My wife had a copy of the list, just in case …

On this list was Ian Pannell, a friend from my BBC days who was in Kabul reporting for ABC News, and Paul Danahar, who had been my boss at the BBC but had since become a dear friend. Some of my professors from Middlebury College in Vermont — Febe Armanious, Hector Vila, and Timi Mayer — were in regular touch, concerned about my safety amid the turmoil. And so were Laurie Patton, president of Middlebury College, and my classmate and friend Sarah Harris.

Like a family, they had all come together, with a fiery resolve to pull me out of the mess.

Ian and ABC News producer Sohel Uddin, who were stationed at the Serena Hotel in downtown Kabul, were also speaking to officials in the Qatari embassy. Now that things had turned ugly, Ian asked me to pack my bags as he arranged a vehicle to drive me to the Serena Hotel.

"We have to leave, *now*," I told my wife bluntly. She was shocked to see my dishevelled state, but she's a smart woman and understood soon what it was all about.

"Can't afford to draw attention," I continued, "so carry just a pair of clothes in a small handbag."

She read the urgency in my words, though it was not that easy to convince my parents.

But a little prodding and a few tears from my better half did the trick!

(The "old friend" from school has been promoted and is now an advisor to the Taliban leadership. The house in Kabul still stands but is in a mess, trashed by Taliban patrols upset at not finding what they came looking for.)

A Refugee in My Own Land

What's good about hitting the bottom, it is said, is that there's only one way to go. In my case, the way led straight to the Hamid Karzai International Airport. For anyone desperate to leave Afghanistan, the airport was the only exit gate. But the Taliban had taken control of all the roads leading to the airport. A holding area was thus needed to gather the wits and wait for that golden opportunity.

As a secure sanctuary from violence, there wasn't a place more bitterly appropriate than the Serena Hotel.

The stunning ultra-luxury hotel had been the site of some of the most brutal terrorist assaults in Kabul, including the 1979 killing of the U.S. ambassador to Afghanistan, Adolph Dubs. During the civil war, it was heavily damaged, but was renovated and reopened in 2005. In 2008, Taliban attacked the hotel when the Norwegian foreign minister was staying there, killing six people. In 2014, a mass shooting in the hotel's restaurant killed nine civilians.

The Serena Hotel was a favourite with foreign tourists, wealthy Afghans, and high-ranking officials until the Taliban overran Kabul. Now the preferred venue of the Taliban's daily press briefings, it also housed the embassy of Qatar.

The presence of the Qatari ambassador to Afghanistan, Saeed bin Mubarak Al-Khayarin, provided a protective layer to the Serena Hotel: the Taliban would do nothing to risk their friendship with the Gulf emirate that had hosted the Taliban leadership for more than a decade and was a key player in their negotiations with the West.

Chris, the security advisor for ABC News, waited anxiously for us on a road near the Serena Hotel. He tightly hugged me. Though meeting for the first time, we were supposed to act as though we were good old friends, lest we arouse the suspicion of the Taliban guards posted outside the hotel. Forewarned, we avoided eye contact with the guards as Chris quickly escorted us in.

Inside was a different world altogether.

Light music played in the background as smartly dressed stewards carried trays full of warmth with calm and poise. Small groups of people, refugees in their own country like me, I guess, huddled together in the lobby and foyers. In one corner of the elegant main hall, along the large bay windows, a lavish buffet was laid out, which was frequented by Taliban guards who gleefully chomped on the free food as if there was going to be no tomorrow.

We were taken straight to our rooms and asked, very politely by Chris, not to step out unless explicitly told. "And, of course, no phone calls," he said.

There were more reasons than one for things to go wrong, so it was important to maintain utmost secrecy.

"We are arranging for your exit with the Qataris," Chris said as I checked in to my room.

In the U.S., my college professor Febe Armanious and classmate Sarah Harris had by now petitioned several congresspeople and senators, requesting them to use their influence with the Qatari government to secure my evacuation.

Although I was approved for a visa to enter Canada, there were no direct flights to Toronto. So, an airlift evacuation to an emergency processing centre in a third country, such as Qatar, was the only option.

But for now, it was just a long wait.

On the Edge

Two days and a long night later, I was told to come down to the hotel lobby.

"Your exit has been cleared by the Taliban leadership as well as the government of Qatar," an official of Qatar embassy organising the evacuation told me. "But there is no guarantee."

This was because the Qatari diplomats were struggling to deal with a new headache. The Taliban leaders, it seemed, were losing control over their battlefield commanders and foot soldiers, who manned the checkpoints on roads leading to the airport. And these foot soldiers were particularly hostile to Afghans trying to flee the country.

Besides, there was the looming threat of an attack by Islamic State's Afghan affiliate, the Islamic State-Khorasan or IS-K. Made up mainly of disgruntled Taliban fighters, IS-K had ideological differences with the Taliban and posed a serious challenge to Taliban authority in Afghanistan.

There were fears that IS-K militants had infiltrated the Taliban ranks and could pass information on the movement of buses carrying Afghans to the airport — or worse, they might already have been among the people, waiting for the right moment to carry out a suicide attack.

In the hotel lobby and hall, groups of nervous Afghans had begun to gather. Most were young women and men, some with children in tow. There were many familiar faces: journalists, TV hosts, former officials, and rights defenders — once the opinion-makers of Afghan society but today unwanted in their own country.

Occasional eye contact or a rare smile were replacements for conversation.

The Qatari officials patiently checked the documents of each Afghan hoping to fly out that day, which was followed by a thorough body and baggage search.

"The convoy will leave tonight. Pray all goes well," one official announced, provoking tears as well as sighs of relief.

By the time five minibuses lined up in the porch of the Serena Hotel, it was one a.m. on August 22.

Qatar's ambassador Al-Khayarin — who had by then helped hundreds of Afghans flee to safety — was personally present to once again lead the convoy through Kabul.

The ambassador's motorcade piloted the convoy, which was escorted from the rear by armed Taliban guards riding in two pickup trucks.

It was pitch-dark outside. Inside, absolute silence. An elderly woman sobbed quietly holding her hands together as a little girl sitting beside tried to comfort her.

Just then, out of nowhere, a young Afghan jumped into the bus, triggering a commotion. The man was waving a piece of paper that he thought entitled him to board the bus and eventually fly out of Afghanistan. But no one had the patience or the will to listen. He was quickly deboarded in a manner not-so-civil.

The Taliban had set up checkpoints at every street corner of Kabul, forcing the convoy to halt as soldiers with contemptuous looks scanned the passengers with their penetrating eyes. At almost every checkpoint, the Qatari ambassador as well as the Taliban escort had to intervene. The convoy finally reached the airport at four thirty a.m., taking three-and-a-half hours for a journey that would have normally taken not more than fifteen minutes.

(In the following days, there were at least two suicide bombings around the airport in Kabul, which killed nearly two hundred people.)

A Mad Rush

It was madness at the airport. Thousands of Afghans jostled on the narrow road leading to the airport gate. Toddlers, teenagers, mothers with babies, young and old — all pressed tight against each other like cattle in a pen.

Days before, the airport had seen heart-wrenching scenes of Afghans clinging to the wheels of departing planes in their desperation to escape the Taliban, only to fall to their deaths moments later.

While the Taliban manned the access to the airport, inside, the U.S. marines held control, with both firing occasionally in the air to instil some order in the milling crowd.

At some points, the U.S. marines and Taliban fighters stood less than two metres apart, even working together to secure the passage for would-be refugees — a reflection of the tragic irony of war.

After about twenty minutes of negotiations at the gate, the convoy was let in, filling the air with joy.

But a thought wavered to those on the other side of the airport and the young man we had all pushed out of the bus. A sudden emptiness enveloped me. Helpless myself, I could only pray for them.

The buildings inside the airport were all taken up by troops — U.S. and other countries who were now arriving in hordes. We had to wait out in the scorching sun.

Qatari officials served water, juice, and snacks as never-ending lines of Afghans boarded one military aircraft after another.

As I sat on the tarmac, my life flashed before me. Twenty years earlier — just when a passenger plane crashed into the World Trade Center in New

York, followed by another one — I was an Afghan refugee boy selling carpets to gullible westerners at a fake antique shop in Peshawar, Pakistan.

My Afghan origins and command over Pashto and Dari, and a working knowledge of English, helped me get a job as a "fixer" with Abu Dhabi TV, whose crew was keen to crossover into Afghanistan and report on the ensuing war. From there to ABC News and then to the BBC, one small step at a time had shaped me into what I was.

Over the following years, my travels to the remote interior of Afghanistan and its frontlines gave me a unique perspective on the life of ordinary Afghans even as it forged my own identity in Afghan soil. But now, destiny was about to snatch this identity. I was going to be a refugee once again.

Most of the planes landing at the airport were empty, but one had a group of foreign correspondents on board. I spotted among them Lyse Doucet, my old friend and the BBC's chief international correspondent.

"Bilal, you were always the one who said, I will never leave Afghanistan," Lyse said as I slowly trudged up the line towards a waiting C-17 military transport plane.

She was right. I had never imagined that I would be at the crossroads once again, with empty pockets and a broken heart.

"My love affair with Afghanistan is fatal," I told her.

I have buried my dreams, but I have not lost hope ... not yet.

"I will be back."

A torrent of tears broke the barrier as the C-17 took off.

(This is a factual account. Some names and descriptions of people have been changed to protect their identity.)

Luis Horacio Nájera
(Mexico)

LUIS HORACIO NÁJERA is an award-winning journalist who fled to Canada in 2008 after receiving death threats for reporting on drug cartels and corruption along the U.S.-Mexico border. Despite completing two master's degrees, publishing in national newspapers, and co-authoring three books while in exile, Nájera still struggles with unemployment.

INTRODUCTION

Luis Horacio Nájera has been exiled in Canada since 2008. His awards include the 2010 CJFE International Press Freedom Award and the 2011 Human Rights Watch Hellman/Hammett Award.

Mexico is one of the world's most dangerous countries for journalists. Between 2000 and 2020, human rights and press freedom organizations reported 159 journalists killed because of their work. The author personally met twelve of those victims.

Success?

~I~

FOUR YEARS AGO, I deleted my Facebook account.

Honestly, there was too much success among my virtual friends for me to handle, one post at the time. Between prosperous businesses, professional achievements, or paradisiacal vacations, the global showcase of social media simply became an emotional burden too heavy for me to carry. For good or for bad, we live in a world flooded by tweets, likes, and shares constantly reminding those on the other side of the screen that there is a place, a job, or a status to enjoy, to conquer, to publish. For me, a journalist surviving in exile since 2008, the permanent feed of smiles, promotions, travels, and accomplishments became a constant reminder of how inadequate I am, according to Canadian society, at successfully reinventing myself in my new country.

I opened my Facebook account months before fleeing Mexico. I did it mainly for journalistic purposes rather than as a new channel for interacting with old or making new friends. It was a new resource for accessing information, contacting sources, and monitoring both sides of the U.S.-Mexico border, the region where I worked as senior correspondent for *Grupo Reforma*, one of the most influential newspapers in the country. In those early days of social media, my network was real rather than virtual; it was extensive, and it was supportive. Relatives, friends, and even members of the church I attended were always around when we needed them, as happened after my daughter was born. Since my wife required a c-section, both mother and baby stayed a few days at the clinic with my mother-in-law taking care of them; meanwhile, energetic members of the church volunteered — without us asking them — to clean our house and cook delicious meals for me and my two sons until the recently extended female section of the family returned.

Furthermore, both my wife and I had well-paying jobs that allowed us to afford a decent mortgage for a house in a middle-class neighbourhood, located at walking distance from the chapel where we both served in volunteer leadership positions. She, as president of the adult women's group, frequently travelled across the city with her two counsellors and our baby daughter to assist in spiritual and temporal needs. Meanwhile, I was one of the twelve men in the advising committee to the local presidency, overseeing around fifteen hundred members, many of them living in poor neighbourhoods I regularly visited. On weekdays, I reported and photographed cartel-related violence in the beginning of Mexico's "war on drugs"; on Sundays, I returned and stood at pulpits to share messages of hope and faith.

In those days, I succeeded economically, spiritually, and professionally. I knew it, and the people I cared about also knew it without posting it, sharing it, or photographing it. However, things dramatically changed for me and my family when, under death threats because of my reporting on corruption, violence, and drug cartels, we fled to Vancouver to begin a new life that inadvertently brought a new relationship with social media and its embedded notion of success.

~II~

In addition to deficient insulation, a malfunctioning furnace, and a lack of furniture, the old two-storey, three-bedroom, semi-detached house we rented in the suburbs through our guarantor — our new church leader — always felt cold, except for one corner in the laundry room. It wasn't warm because of the heat generated by the dryer; it felt warm because that was the only spot to get a weak, yet free, Wi-Fi signal that allowed us to connect with family and friends via the then popular MSN Messenger. That corner was our gateway to the human, social network we had left behind.

In 1954, Canadian anthropologist Kalervo Oberg coined the term "culture shock" to describe the changes in our value systems when exposed to new ideas in a new country. Oberg also outlined five stages of culture shock lived by immigrants: Honeymoon, Rejection, Regression, Recovery or At-Ease-At-Last, and Reverse Culture Shock or Return Culture Shock. Based on my own experience, I can say that those stages are real; however, there have been some changes to them for good and for bad since the emergence of social media. The Honeymoon stage, or the initial excitement that comes when discovering a new country, culture, and lifestyle, has been amplified by the internet. Either YouTube, Instagram, or Facebook are permanent canvases for newcomers to expose their new life, a significant achievement if moving was a change for good. Hence, each post, vlog, or photo becomes a record of personal success worth sharing with the world.

Not for me.

After our arrival in Canada, I took hundreds of photos with the Sony Ericsson smartphone I had kept from Mexico. I did it not because I wanted to share the joy of moving to a beautiful city; I did it because I was building a digital memory for my posterity. The generations that follow me need to know how their ancestors ended up here, and how many challenges we faced, and how long we endured while living in exile. In those days, my virtual connection with family and friends was through shared folders in Google Photos where I displayed my own version of the honeymoon stage, which basically was enjoying surviving death threats and being alive. After a few months in Vancouver, and through my former co-worker and photography mentor, Miguel Cervantes, I upgraded my equipment by trading him my phone for a small digital Nikon camera that allowed me to increase my collection of memories. As Facebook became more popular, I used it more to communicate with relatives in Mexico, sharing with them photos of marvellous places as a way to hide our struggles, as well as a resource for connecting with the people from our new church congregation in the suburbs that became our hybrid network: online friends, real-life acquaintances.

Research shows that after some time in a new country, newcomers transition into the Rejection phase of cultural shock, which is when they realize that nothing is as beautiful, perfect, or efficient as initially perceived. Based on what I have seen, the internet and social media have also altered this stage, leading newcomers to create both a *virtual* persona and a real personality. I did it. I had to, because I thought it wouldn't be pleasant for my family in Mexico to view my posts about our challenges and disgraces, such as the time when someone broke into our house and stole all our food — the only thing we had worth stealing. Instead, I chose to show them colourful gardens, majestic buildings, and impressive mountains. Other immigrants who came to Canada looking for economic prosperity are motivated to hide their struggles and exaggerate their successes out of vanity rather than concern for anxiety back home.

In addition to the reality check that comes during the Rejection stage, constantly thinking about the good things available only in your old country is a significant component of the second phase in the process of culture shock. For me, thirteen years after fleeing Mexico, thoughts and even dreams of me working as a journalist at the U.S.-Mexico border are still frequent, particularly after being bombarded by social media with posts, shares, and likes about former colleagues being promoted, hired, awarded, or even retired. It is still really hard for me to move away from it because I'm not there, thriving on my photography and my writing. Instead, I am here, frequently unemployed, constantly depressed, and regularly ignored.

When a newcomer spends too much time struggling within the Rejection phase, Regression could be the natural consequence. Social isolation from those who are not from your own background, increased anxiety, and regret about leaving your country of origin may lead to repatriation, unless adaptation and settlement — the Recovery or At-Ease-At-Last stage of culture shock — make life easier. Again, the internet and social media altered the process by changing the mindset of immigrants. The more you post about your accomplishments, the more you believe in yourself, the better you feel, the more you adapt and settle. This may be dangerous territory because hiding your struggles while developing somehow a social/personal dependency on selfies, likes, and shares could lead to deeper crisis in the long term. Perhaps that's what happened to me at some point in my relationship with social media, exile, and success.

~III~

It would be dishonest of me to not recognize the moments of success, both virtual and real, I have experienced in Canada. The first was receiving refugee status. It took me countless nights of researching and printing hundreds of pages to assemble an extensive file of three booklets of supporting evidence that, according to the Immigration and Refugee Board, irrefutably justified granting me and my family protection. Of course, as soon as we left the building after the hearing, I posted on Facebook with an update on my status: *feeling happy*. Equally shared were the two international awards I received: one in Canada and one in the United States, both granted in recognition of the dire circumstances I endured while working as a journalist in Mexico.

Also, dozens of posts and hundreds of photos uploaded between August 2011 and June 2014 displayed what for me had been the happiest years in Canada so far: moving to Toronto; joining Massey College as a Journalism Fellow; meeting some of Canada's greatest minds; travelling to Europe twice; making new friends; watching my older son leave home and serve at a church mission for two years while his younger siblings thrived at school; my wife improving her English; and finally becoming Canadian citizens. All of this was shared online because each post somehow meant redemption after years of struggling and scrubbing floors as a janitor in Vancouver. Furthermore, the pinnacle of my virtual success was letting the cyberworld know of my graduation as a Master of Global Affairs from the University of Toronto, completing a program that enhanced my endurance as I climbed up the steepest learning curve of my life. Status: *feeling successful*.

Reflecting on choices made after my graduation, I recognize that between the hype of constantly posting on social media, becoming a Canadian citizen, and my recent academic degree, my judgment got clouded by excitement and pride. In addition, I erroneously perceived that, after years of invisibility, I had successfully earned a place within "the system" as an educated, experienced professional with the legal, moral, and academic rights to finally enjoy the fruits of this land of milk and honey. In my mind, once I cleared the citizenship and higher education barriers, my possibilities for getting a good job that would bring prosperity and stability for me and my family would increase significantly. In my mind, I was finally one of them, both virtually and physically.

Big, big mistake.

From time to time, life cracks a joke on you. That happened when I was hired as content editor for a new digital project in one of Canada's most influential newspapers. Again, I flooded my social media with posts and photos about my new job, the newsroom, and the joy of being a journalist-sort-of again. After six months of working there, I was asked to write an op-ed about the meeting between actor Sean Penn and Joaquin "El Chapo" Guzmán; a few days later, I was interviewed for a piece on the Scholars-at-Risk fund that I received while studying my master's degree; the next day, my op-ed was published and prompted a live interview on TV to speak about it. So, this is how success feels, eh?

Thinking that I was finally one of them, I planned to ask for an opportunity to write a monthly column on Latin American issues, and maybe later to pitch some stories that I could report in collaboration.

Maybe in the future I could go back to being a reporter, a writer, a photojournalist again. Maybe I get that back into my life, I fantasized while riding the subway on a Thursday night, checking on my phone for updates on how many new comments, likes, and shares I got after posting on my Facebook profile the video of my TV interview.

The very next morning, life laughed at me as I left the newsroom in shock after being notified that I had lost my job, while my profile still collected happy face and thumbs-up emojis in response to my latest publication.

~IV~

Among the many workshops, seminars, and conversations I took part in as an immigrant on how to find a job in Canada, having and using effectively a network was always highlighted as essential to succeed. Furthermore, using social media and dedicated websites such as LinkedIn to connect with people in the chosen field is essential. Equally essential is to let the world know about the hiring, the promotion, or the award you get, because that post, that virtual announcement, means you are successful in your new country; it means that you are indeed living the Canadian dream.

So far, I have used LinkedIn once to successfully connect with a specialist in a different field I considered as an option to start over in Canada. I chose her because she also has a background in journalism and eventually left and moved into her new field of expertise. Through that common past, we connected and began a good friendship that, after her advice, led me to enroll in my second master's program at York University, where I had to create a new Facebook account in order to connect with my classmates and professors. However, this new digital persona remained "hidden" from previous contacts, both personal and professional. I guess I did learn from my previous mistakes by keeping posting to the minimum, and basically only school-related content that still remains in the cloud without further interaction.

Meanwhile, LinkedIn continues bombarding my email every week, letting me know how many people have found, some of them seen, and probably a few actually scrolled down my profile's screen to learn about who I am.

I still don't know why such a narrative of success hasn't worked out for me. My checklist of possibilities for failure is extensive: my age, my education, my ethnicity, my previous experience, my thick accent, my deficient writing in English, my introverted character, my physical appearance, or my lack of online followers may be factors that eventually led me to continue to be unemployed, even after getting a second master's degree from York. Since I couldn't change my accent, my age, or my background, I found that the only immediate change I could make was to delete my

Facebook account. Why? Because each post depressed me and reminded me of how "the system," whatever it is in Canada, considers me unworthy of it. Likewise, social media constantly bombarded me with successful stories, images, and videos of people I met while in Mexico; they survived horror and moved forward while I am still here, daydreaming of getting a full-time job and hoping for a real-life update that permanently gives me my human dignity back.

~V~

After graduating from my first master's program, I felt the urgency to acquire more knowledge; hence, I committed myself to read between forty to fifty-two books per year. My goal was to read at least one book a week, depending on its number of pages, topic, and availability at thrift stores, garage sales, bookstore clearances, and donations. Moreover, since I do live in Canada, I decided that the majority of the literature to be intellectually consumed should be in English, and mostly by anglophone writers, as a way to accelerate my language skills and my understanding of how "the system" works.

So far, I have not completed my goal due to unpredictable, opportunistic episodes of despair that from time-to-time ambush me in the middle of my readings, thus beginning a fierce battle for control of my emotions and attention that is frequently won by my invisible adversary. And yet, my determination to expand my vision of the world and my stubbornness to keep fighting for me, my wife, my children, and my daughter-in-law continues.

For a refugee, being stubborn is a grey zone that eventually could define your future in your new country. There is indeed a fine balance — it's almost an art itself to decide when to keep pushing and when to resist moving and, at least for me, it is still a work in progress.

I vividly recall the first meeting with our assigned case worker a few weeks after we arrived in Vancouver in 2008. After asking me about my professional background in Mexico she energetically said, "Forget that; you would never be a journalist in Canada, ever. Instead, I do have some courses on carpentry, cooking, forklift operator, or residential painter to help you to settle and begin a new life here."

An awkward silence.

In October 2021, after three years of research, and significant setbacks caused by my wife's cancer treatment, and later a global pandemic, our book *The Wolfpack: The Millennial Mobsters Who Brought Chaos and the Cartels to the Canadian Underworld* was finally published by Random House of Canada in English and later by Les Editions De L'Homme in French. Co-authored with Peter Edwards, one of the best crime reporters in the country and one of the most generous, compassionate, and smart Canadians I have ever met, our book is a testament to my stubbornness in taking the road less travelled, the one that patiently privileges extended human interactions rather than immediate posts or virtual — and frequently hollow — online friendships, such as most of those I had on that Facebook account I deleted four years ago.

Kaziwa Salih, Ph.D.
(Kurdistan-Iraq)

KAZIWA SALIH is an anthropologist who holds a Ph.D. in Cultural Studies from Queen's University in Canada with a focus on the cultural sociology of genocidal violence against the Kurds in Iraq. After publishing a predictive article about the emergence of Islamic radicalism such as ISIS in her magazine *Nivar*, Salih was imprisoned by the Kurdish authorities. On her release, she fled the country.

She is the award-winning author of several fiction and non-fiction books. Salih was a founder and editor-in-chief of two journals, *Nivar* and *Newkar*. Her research interests include Genocide Studies, Cultural-Sociology and Cultural-Psychology of Violence, Migration and Displacement, Kurdish Studies, Middle East Politics and Women's Identity, Ethnic Conflicts, State and Non-State Actors, and Yazidi Affairs.

Feeding Her Child a Green Slipper
Instead of a Cucumber

I FIRST OBSERVED Nabat Fayiaq Rahman's confident, sad, yet hopeful face on the screen of my television. She was dressed in a traditional black Kurdish outfit that matched the stage curtains created for the April 14 commemoration of the Anfal genocide. In the 1980s, Saddam Hussein's regime committed the genocide of the Kurdish Anfal in Iraq. Human Rights Watch (1994) estimates that 182,000 Kurds were buried alive in mass graves, many of which were discovered after Saddam Hussein's ouster. More than 2.5 million people were displaced, 4,500 villages were destroyed, and 250 cities and villages were exposed to chemical weapons.

Nabat was from one of the destroyed villages in the Qadir Karam district of the province of Kirkuk. Her angry voice did not match her red eyes, which indicated she had been crying throughout the entire event. "What did the government do for us?" she asked. "They did nothing. Once a year, during the anniversary, they [the government] remember that the Anfal genocide happened."

Nabat's voice disappeared into a chorus of female voices sorrowfully singing a heartfelt lament, which until that moment had been playing quietly in the background of the program.

Lullaby, lullaby, lullaby.
The grief of the Kurds makes me lose my voice.
To sing a lament for all of you, each one thrice.
Lament for my burning soul that doesn't rest day or night.
Lullaby, for my sons

Lullaby, for my daughters
Lament for my husband, who was a leading word
A lament for my parents
Lament for my sisters.
Lullaby, for my brother, who was my word.
Lullaby for neighbours who turned to ash
Sleep, my loved ones.
May you find peace in the grave.
Since the Earth is a slaughtering cave.

A lullaby is a prominent piece of art in Kurdish society and a means by which the female survivors of the Kurdish genocides can express their anguish since they don't have access to psychiatric treatment. However, I am against treating the five Kurdish genocides with only lullabies and speeches. The Kurdish genocides require serious attention that should go beyond singing lullabies and expressing emotions.

The women's lullaby reverberated in my ear. I don't know if it was the lyrics, or if my mind had made up its own lullaby because I'd been hearing them ever since I was a child. Historically, Kurdish culture is known for many different types of lullabies: to send children to sleep, to mend lovers' broken hearts, to record oral history, to pass on classic stories of wisdom. But it has been a century since the lullaby turned mainly into a dark lament for the deceased person too, especially during the anniversary of the Kurdish genocides.

The women who survived the Kurdish Anfal genocide are mostly isolated and clad in black outfits — the isolation and the outfits have been part of the villagers' culture for over thirty years. Among them, a few elderly survivors attend the genocide events so as to perform lullabies and make audiences weep. Nabat's presence on TV was impressive. In the culturally conservative and male-dominated society of the villages, survivors have chosen silence over speech, and some of them refuse to tell their stories, even anonymously, due to cultural and psychological burdens. A bud of hope grew and sucked out some of my unwelcomed tears that I'd been harbouring about myself, namely, "Why can't I stop my tears whenever I see or hear the wailing and lament of a wounded person? Don't you think that is a metaphor for self-re-victimization?"

Unlike Nabat, I've wiped away my tears and managed to fake a smile while reminding myself that here is an illiterate widow, a single mother of several children, victimized by one of the most ferocious events in history, not only telling her story but participating in a conference on the Kurdish genocide in Iraq, criticizing and fighting the government about the rights of the Anfal genocide survivors.

That day, I wrote down her full name and the name of her region, making a promise to myself that I would go all the way to Kurdistan, if only to see her.

In August 2015, I went to Kurdistan — specifically to conduct field work on the sexual enslavement of Yazidi women by the Islamic State of Iraq and Syria (ISIS), but I had Nabat in mind too. Habil Ahmad, a general manager of the Directorate of Anfal Monument in Chamchamal, had arranged my transportation and for me to meet Nabat at her home in Bani Gul village.

Seeing the village's yellowish landscapes from the window of the car, especially in that hot weather, triggered a bittersweet mix of childhood memories. I felt a sudden, sharp pain in my thigh as if something hard were poking at my body from below. To examine the contents of my seat, I shifted to the middle seat, which was empty. Without any luck, I recalled Elaine Scarry's book *The Body in Pain*, in which she discusses how a torture victim's recollections of that ordeal can resurrect and intensify the pain they felt. After giving it some thought, I concluded that my body had retrieved a particularly unpleasant memory. Scarry focused exclusively on the political repercussions of premeditated suffering; she made no assertions regarding how social ramification also produces pain.

Those memories have nothing to do with the destruction of the Kurdish villages, but with my family's persecution by the Ba'ath party, and that is what I remember most vividly. My father was imprisoned yearly by the Ba'ath regime because he comes from a revolutionary family with four Peshmerga (Kurdish freedom fighters) brothers and because he refused to work for the Ba'ath. To protect my siblings and me from the Ba'athists, my mother would move us to a remote village, much like a mother cat would relocate her kittens to a safer location in the house. One part of going to the village was exciting for me: seeing and playing with animals. At the time, city dwellers were not permitted to keep pets, so this was an unusual experience for me, as was visiting a farm and staying with families who had a variety of animals. The hard part, as a child who didn't understand the financial and environmental problems, was when my father was imprisoned, and my family was forced to go into hiding in the countryside. I had to wake up early every day in order to catch the first car back to school in the city. This way, my classmates and teachers would never know where we were hiding, and I could continue my education without fear of being questioned. This was also a potentially dangerous move, but we were stuck with it.

There would typically be only one car leaving the village for the city, and it would be jam-packed with adults, mostly men, who were making the trip for a variety of reasons. I was the only kid to ever wake up at six a.m. to catch up with these adults and reserve a spot for myself in the car, and I always paid the same fee as the adults. However, I was always told to make room for an adult or elderly passenger, and I usually did so, leaving my seat and sitting on the car wheel in the middle of the car that was in the way of my seat, which was always uncomfortable and painful. Until I finished elementary school, I had this thought at least once a year for a few months. *I wonder if they knew the body has memory, would they have taken my place?* I reflected in silence.

The driver's comment drew my gaze away from the yellow bush on the side road and brought me back to the present. "We're almost there, those houses." He pointed out the window to a row of new, modest, white- and ivory-coloured dwellings whose identical design reminded him of the ghetto. He continued, "In the last few years, these houses were built for the survivors of the Anfal, but they didn't build enough." I was curious as to who they were, but he stopped in front of one of them after asking a child which house was Nabat's home, and he got out while saying, "I have been here a few times, driven a few journalists to her home, but because the houses are undifferentiated and unnumbered, I always get confused."

When we met, as expected, Nabat was fully clad in a traditional black outfit. She said she had been wearing it since 1988 — her untraditional way of attempting to make a difference. This time, her red eyes and hopeless face expressed the unspeakable agonies of a heartbroken woman and mother of seven children who felt that no one understood her pain. My sister Nyan, who had accompanied me on this trip, took a few photos of her.

It is challenging to ask victims to relive the trauma they experienced. After I expressed this concern, Nabat replied, "I want to tell not only the Kurds but the entire world what happened to us; but the problems we suffered during the Anfal cannot be put into words."

Even so, she thought it was worth trying, and recounted how she was captured in April 1988, along with her husband, seven children (four sons and three daughters), four brothers-in-law, and several cousins. The people of her village, she continued, were taken to concentration camps in the south of Iraq.

Nabat was released after six months, "by a miracle," as she calls it, but she lost two of her children in those camps: a seven-year-old son and a three-year-old daughter.

What caused their deaths?

"Hunger and disease," she said. "We were put in a huge barn filled with animal excrement and cockroaches. The barn was full of women and children with no food or drink. Once a day, we were given a piece of bread with a glass of water."

I don't know what it's like to live on nothing but a round muffin's worth of bread and a glass of water every day, but after visiting Auschwitz I and Auschwitz II-Birkenau in 2013, I feel like I've witnessed that kind of concentration camp and the practices of dehumanization and slaughter. During World War II and the Holocaust from 1939 to 1945, Nazi Germany created and ran these camps, subjecting millions of people to forced labour from morning to night with just a meagre ration of food and water to ensure their slow and painful deaths. In commemoration of the victims, the governments of Poland and Germany have preserved the locations as research centres; however, in 2013, I was told that the Negrosalman barns that had been used as concentration camps by the Ba'ath dictatorship for the Anfal victims were once again being used as barns for Arabic horses. In response, I warned that the genocide of the Kurds would continue indefinitely because the genocide against the Kurds began and persisted due to denial.

She choked on her tears. Her eyes were fixed on an abstract point far away, and her arms were locked across her chest while she moved her head back and forth. This went on for a while until her gaze moved to the clock, and suddenly, as if she'd remembered something important, she called out a girl's name. It was 12:20 p.m.

A beautiful teenage girl, Nabat's daughter, entered. After greeting me, she asked her mother if she needed anything. Nabat asked her to prepare lunch for me.

As a member of the community, I already knew about Kurdish etiquette and hospitality: it was expected that I should eat in their home. But I didn't want to be a burden, so I quickly said that I preferred a light meal, perhaps a tomato and cucumber salad.

Silence ensued, and my thoughts wandered to the injustices Nabat had encountered. Despite her anguish, she looked like she couldn't be older than fifty. Since these events had taken place thirty years ago, and she was a mother of seven children, it meant that she must have gotten married when she was little more than a child. Yes, I thought, she was one of the many whose childhood had been stolen from her. When she should have been enjoying the beauty of youth, she had been forced to be a wife and a mother; she had experienced the agony of genocide, losing her loved ones; and she had been a widow who, alone, had to look after five children in a male-dominated society.

I didn't bother confirming her age, and usually don't ask my interviewee's age, because I believe in the axiom "In the end, it's not the years in your life that count; it's the life in your years." In this sense, one needs only to consider the decent times of their life when calculating their age. Kurdish children didn't have a childhood due to all the oppression and aftermath problems within Kurdish society, especially during Nabat's generation. For a moment, I forgot about Nabat. In my mind, I tried to calculate life in the years rather than the years in my life. I came up only with a few months. I thought I would ask my family to write on my grave that my age was only a few months when I died. Then I thought it made no sense to ask Nabat how old she was. If I were her, I would say I haven't been born for life yet.

Between Nabat and me was a traditional Kurdish pillow, ivory with brown flowers and sage leaves. I watched her in silence while she made repeated movements with her index finger, as if pushing the fallen leaf toward the twig of the flower. She was remapping her lost world, I thought. How I too wished we could rejoin the broken branch to her family tree just through the art of finger-pointing.

I looked in my sister Nyan's direction. She seemed engrossed in taking photos. I hoped that she too had noticed Nabat's reaction to the design on the pillow and processed it in the same way I had.

It didn't take long for the tomato and cucumber salad to be placed before me. "You have to eat with me," I told Nabat. I was surprised she didn't start with me; culturally, we don't leave our guest to eat alone.

"No, I don't eat anything that has cucumber."

"Why? Do you have an allergy?"

"I wish," she said, and sighed.

I realized then that the salad hadn't been as effortless to make as I'd thought it would be. I was overcome with guilt.

I learned then that Nabat had not eaten a cucumber for more than thirty years. Cucumbers reminded her of an incident in the concentration camp of Negrosalman when her five-year-old daughter Sharooh had been very sick with a fever and diarrhea like most of the children and elderly people on the premises. Nabat told me that her daughter had been crying continuously and asking for ice and cucumber.

"Imagine that. We couldn't even get water," added Nabat.

Then she grew silent, and tears ran down her cheeks. I gave her the glass of water I was holding. She took gulps of it and continued. "There was a soldier in front of the camp's door. He had a tub of cucumbers in front of him; he and his soldier friends were eating from it. I told him that my child was taking her last breath and was asking for a cucumber. Maybe she smelled it because he was eating it close to our door ... I begged him to give me one," she added. It made the cucumber taste bitter, and an unpleasant feeling travelled from my nose to my stomach, as if I were experiencing postnasal drip. I dropped my fork out of guilt for forcing her to smell and see it.

"He didn't answer at first. Then I again urged him to help — I even told him that my child would die soon. Not for myself," I sobbed, "but for God's sake, let her have a small cucumber, her very last wish!"

Nabat's sobbing grew louder.

Nobody, I thought then and still today, seems to realize that the origin of these brutalities lies in the lack of empathy for "the other," our estrangement from those we deem different and separate from who we are. In fact, I was reminded then of one of the golden rules taught to us in conducting research: that we are not expected to get emotionally involved with our interviewees. What a challenging and seemingly contradictory requirement! Devote yourself wholeheartedly to the pursuit of other people's happiness, rights, and well-being while simultaneously demonstrating that you feel no sympathy for their suffering. I couldn't obey this paradoxical role.

Nabat continued, "The soldier threw a few cucumbers down in front of himself and started smashing them into the ground with his big combat boots." She looked at the floor and shook her head. "I thought my daughter was going to die, and I had to do something to give her a little hope before she left this world. I found a green slipper and put it in her hand. My child believed it was a cucumber and started biting into it. She died a few hours later."

Nabat continued to sob, and after taking a long breath she added, "Only forty days afterwards, my son Diary also died after he got sick."

I was deeply moved. What a strong woman, I thought. Without tampering with the mood and flow of our conversation, I told her, "Now I know why, among hundreds, I was drawn to talk to you: because you're a strong woman and a great mother. You are truly an achiever."

"Not anymore," she replied. "I'm overwhelmed with sorrow."

Nabat confirmed what many other survivors of the Anfal genocide had reported: they didn't have enough tools to dig graves for the people who died in the camps. These victims were merely buried under thin layers of soil. Sometimes, at night, wild dogs from the desert could be heard uncovering and eating the corpses. Being Kurdish means you are familiar with these types of scenes, so I did not recoil at the image of the corpses that were hanging in my imagination.

I thought back to the time I had sent an article to the editor of a European journal, comparing Saddam Hussein to Hitler. I had chosen her for my article because she was an Arab and I believed that, as a Middle Easterner, she would have a deeper understanding of these issues. Even though I had experienced hundreds of acts of bigotry and chauvinism since moving to Canada, not only from Iraqi Arabs but from people from all over the world, I reasoned that, as an academic, she could not be subjective. Again, I was mistaken; she retaliated with vehemence and, like most Arabs, boldly asserted that Saddam Hussein was not comparable to Hitler and defended his crimes.

"Human nature is complex," I murmured. How can a person be so spiteful and justify it? I couldn't agree more with Anurag Shourie who once said, "A weapon is only an extension of one's own persona; as lethal or useless as the person wielding it."

A hard sneeze caused me to jerk and return to the present moment. I then observed the shadow of a person passing by the window and heard him say, "Thank God," after he sneezed. In my mind, I also said, "Thank you for sneezing, because if you hadn't, my memory would have taken me to a multitude of similar incidents. To the journey of suffering and exclusion."

I wanted to ask about her husband, but at that moment she was again staring vacantly outside. After some time, her gaze moved to a nearby wall where there was a pencil sketch of a young man. "Is he your son?" I asked.

"No, it is a picture of my husband."

"How long before the Anfal genocide was that photo taken?"

"Only a few years before the Anfal. This photo was on his, eh, ahm ... identity." She couldn't remember the term "identity card." She added, "A relative redrew it. That is all we have of him."

Obviously, he had been a young parent like Nabat. He too hadn't experienced a proper or fulfilling childhood; his youth may have ended by being buried alive, shot, or killed under torture, or through hunger. He too might have been fed to the stray dogs kept by the Negrosalman concentration camp guards for this particular task. Like so many other victims, his fate would never be known.

It is known that during the genocide, before destroying their victims' homes, perpetrators would loot their property, including jewellery, livestock, and pets. That was why survivors often ended up without tangible histories and memories, deprived of even something as banal as family photos. When they returned, they owned nothing and had nowhere to go. Consequently, the remaining children could not go to school because they lacked the financial means.

"Your husband's history is lost, just like the history of his people," I remarked, my voice vibrating through my body from the emotion as I remembered my own experiences of losing the history.

"We have all lost our history," Nabat said. "We have not only lost our loved ones but even the photos of them we could have looked at."

I paused for a while, mulling over whether I should tell her about my experiences.

Finally, I said, "I know what it's like to be without a family history." I felt guilt, remorse, and embarrassment. "The Ba'ath imprisoned my father almost every year. Most of the time, my mother would take the children — my siblings and me — to one of the villages so she could protect us from being put in prison. Often when we would return, belongings from our home would have been looted or confiscated. I don't have anything from my childhood. No one in my family has any signs or evidence of our history. I have always wished to have a photo from my childhood."

A wound on one's memory lasts longer than any other type of wound. Indeed, events do come to an end, but some memories last forever.

I sat quietly, and an unbidden memory from elementary school came to mind. A few classmates had decided to share their childhood photos with one another. Some of them were my best friends, and they had all assumed I'd be part of this activity.

But I didn't have any photos — let alone a doll or a toy — to remind me of my childhood.

It may sound simple, but it never is. Not when a child returns to her mother, now an older woman, and asks her to prove she was once a child, her child. What if that child suddenly exclaims that she couldn't possibly be that woman's child, because if she was, then where are the toys, childhood photos, and other memorabilia?

I didn't need to be a scholar to know that rape was a tool of genocide and war. Since I started working on the genocide of the Kurds, I've been interested in questions of rape and sexual assault against victimized women.

I've tried to broach this subject several times so as to gain confirmation that the women of the Anfal were indeed rape and sexual assault victims. I had wanted to understand how they dealt with the consequences of sexual assault, but I had always been pushed away by male family members of victims, or by male directors of genocide institutions.

Now it was important for me, I thought, to ask Nabat — this brave widow here in this small village — whether she had witnessed these atrocities in concentration camps. Or maybe it would be wiser to delay asking the question till the end just in case it affected her mood. The question was one I was hesitant to ask: asking a victim to recount their experience of victimization in a society that holds victims responsible for their own suffering and turns their experiences of victimization into perpetual processes.

Questioning the victim, I've long concluded, isn't half as difficult as thinking about Kurdish scholars' and feminists' positions regarding victimized women. It's disappointing, in fact, that in scholarly books on Kurdish women who've been victims of the Anfal genocide, especially in gender studies, the women have never been asked about being raped. This is why victims have never been able to seek counselling.

Nabat didn't like my question. It made her uncomfortable. She looked to her right, and her upper-right lip twitched twice. Then, reluctantly, she said, "I don't know. In the concentration camps, we never talked about it. But sometimes, the soldiers would take the ladies who were young and beautiful and return them a few hours later. They were sad, and they grew more withered day after day. We didn't ask them — after all, we all had enough on our plates — but we also knew that those women were raped."

It was the same answer that my Aunt Rabia, my mother's sister, had given me years ago. (She had been released after almost two years because she was elderly.) I had also heard the same story from another relative who was from Garmin.

The similarities of these accounts were undeniable, and clearly, it was a confirmation of what I'd thought all along.

The cultural practice of wearing black to mourn the death of a loved one has always tormented me. In my book *Feminism and Kurdish Society* (2005), I explored the psychological consequences of this dark culture. However, writing for the undereducated, traumatized class of society is worthless if activist groups don't transmit and convert academic or theoretical ideas into a practical, digestible form through counselling and hands-on workshops.

Now, as our interview was ending, I asked Nabat, "Do you know that the black outfit you wear creates more of a psychological burden?"

"What can I say?" Nabat answered. "Inside, everything is black for me. I can't wear colours. No one does. All the Anfal survivors are still wearing black."

I had suspected this question of mine would lead nowhere.

Yet I reflected that, despite everything, Nabat had managed to raise her five children to be healthy and strong. She is now one of the bold voices of the survivors. To tell her story, she participates in local, national, and international conferences.

"I've been to Europe a few times for conferences," she asserted. "Despite all the difficulties I'm going through, I don't mind going wherever I can to defend the rights of the victims. Unfortunately, some Kurds don't respect anything," Nabat said, shaking her head. Suddenly, her lips locked tightly, as if she regretted what she had said. I knew what she meant: no one understands each other better than people with similar experiences.

After a while, she mentioned that instead of attracting help and encouragement, she has sometimes been accused of making money out of her horrifying experience. "But I don't pay attention to these people who have no empathy."

Due to ongoing confrontations between Kurds and Arabs and locally between two ruling political parties, the Patriotic Union of Kurdistan (PUK) and the Kurdistan Democratic Party (KDP), the genocide issue has been largely ignored by the Iraqi and Kurdistan authorities. Some irresponsible supporters of these parties, particularly the PUK, which both I and Nabat from that zone oppose, criticize the impartiality of independent genocide scholars and activists. In my experience, I was always criticized by these parties and their many supporters for serving victims and working on a topic that didn't bring me revenue. In Nabat's experience, people believe she is paid to be an activist, and the list of accusations continues to grow, leaving victims and non-partisan scholars in limbo. "I congratulate you on your determination," I replied. "Ignore what they're saying, and don't look back — go forward!"

For the first time, a smile lit up her face. I asked her about what she wanted to achieve and where she wished to be heard.

Nabat said, "If the United Nations, and international community, knew about our stories and our current conditions, they wouldn't accept them. They would punish the Iraqi government and those Kurdish individuals who don't care about our victimization."

The mention of the United Nations reared a lightning strike of a memory that prevented me from breathing properly. I thought to myself, *she must be kidding. The United Nations? No one but the United Nations?* I hoped she didn't find out I used to be a vice president of the United Nations Association of Canada Toronto Branch (UNACTO).

Sometimes I get the impression that no one believes in so-called humanitarian organizations, especially the United Nations, more than Kurds. Observing the entire nation's false optimism regarding these types of institutions makes me feel like a member of a barely alive imaginative community. Yet, I reasoned, the hero must have false hope, even if he or she must die by the end of the film. I promised her that one day I would tell her about the United Nations and why I left UNACTO, but at a time when waking her from her dream wouldn't cause her to fall into a disappointing ditch.

I let her dream — in fact, she was asking the international community to create an agency that could stop this kind of crime in the hopes that no one else would experience what she had gone through. Nabat wanted her voice to help guarantee a safer future for her children. "If we, as victims, don't tell our stories, who is going to make our voices heard?" she finished.

I didn't want to disappoint her further by revealing what I knew to be the true face of the international community. I hugged her goodbye tightly, but my mind didn't stop connecting her belief in the human rights organizations and international community. For the first time, I was happy that Nabat Fayiaq Rahman was illiterate and wouldn't be able to read my words. If she'd asked me in 2017 where I would publish her story, what should I have said? Could I have told her the truth? For instance:

— Nabat, for three years, the mainstream Canadian media have rejected publishing your 700-word story with the excuse that it's not current and not relevant to Canadian society. Rejection of your story, Nabat, suggests that although people of your community hold Canadian passports, they are not considered Canadians, and the grief of their slaughter is meaningless to Canadian society.

— Nabat, I have contacted several feminist media outlets, but they called your story too dark and heavy for their readers' hearts, and they don't want to lose their readers. One of them even asked me to write a weekly column, but on condition that I tell only those stories that can turn women's issues into lucrative businesses that could sell products on Amazon.

— Nabat, there are no problems that occur in the world without the permission of the international community. They had to have known your story even before it happened.

Or should I just tell Nabat that the international community against genocide consists only of a few organizations and some genocide studies scholars? Even these scholars can't magnify her voice if her own people and government won't come forward — something that has not happened in at least the last three decades.

Just like your people, Nabat, your voice is without a homeland. Continue with your sorrowful lullaby, for it is the only true weapon, the only true balm you have before you lose your voice.

Half of this story was published in Genocide Studies and Prevention: An International Journal: *Vol. 15: Issue. 1: 13–21.*

Pedro A. Restrepo
(Colombia)

PEDRO A. RESTREPO is a published writer, journalist, poet, and entrepreneur who won national recognition in literature and art, granted by Colombia's Ministry of Education in 2002. From a very early age, he loved reading and writing. He also loved learning about new cultures and soon became proficient in several languages including English, German, Italian, and French. He fled his beloved Colombia with his family when his father was murdered for his political beliefs.

INTRODUCTION

After its independence from Spain, Colombia experienced violent struggles for possession of the fertile lands once owned by the Spanish feudal lords. When the Spanish crown's troops were ousted, in many regions, rich local landowners took over large extensions of productive land from the peasantry, leaving most without their livelihood. This continued through the nineteenth and twentieth centuries when right-wing, state-sponsored paramilitary groups were created to control the population that was demanding reform. The situation was exacerbated by the assassination of a populist leader named Jorge Eliécer Gaitán in 1948. Gaitán had promised structural reforms in land ownership. After his assassination, peasants formed guerrilla factions demanding social reform. Conflict between these factions and the government's paramilitary groups continued for fifty years. Drug cartels emerged, and both sides accumulated vast financial resources through narcotics and money laundering. This allowed them to acquire more weapons and led to an increase in violence and war crimes, and the displacement of much of the population.

Urabá, the region where I grew up, was just one of the many examples of that inequality, and American multinationals operated in the region hand in hand with local landowners to exploit the fertile lands and resources. My father owned two small farms and was very aware of the problem, and also very vocal about it, which might have led to his assassination and our eventual displacement.

One Life, Two Perspectives

AS FAR BACK as I can remember, I have felt as an explorer who is amazed by every simple detail life has to offer. Whether a sunset or a traffic jam, every happening in our lives has something magic that can make our day, if that is what we want.

With that childish mindset I walked with my father through the vast, humid, and endless plains of banana growing fields that rolled on through thousands of hectares and made me feel they were the only thing there was on Earth. There, in the north of Colombia, was where I grew up and probably lived the happiest years of my childhood.

It was a place like no other, with burning sun and moisture, characteristic of a tropical and jungle-like paradise that seemed to offer all sorts of surprises at every turn of the road. You could see venomous serpents, colourful insects, and spectacular dawns every time you blinked your eyes.

My house was there, in the middle of nowhere, and surrounded by all the fruit trees you can think of — lemons, guavas, soursops, and colourful bushes the snakes used to nest in to avoid the sun and the heat.

It was a simple brick country house that I considered my kingdom. I lived there with my parents — an agronomist and a teacher — and my two brothers. The days went by very quickly with games, school, and sports. The house was part of a camp built by a multinational company to attract professionals of different fields to help keep up with the production demand. They offered comfortable housing and schools, and amenities that you could only find in fancy clubs of the main cities. That was the place where I grew up, protected by the local army and well-armed private security guards from attacks of the guerrillas that operated outside the fences.

As I grew older, I became aware of the widespread inequality that, sadly, was the hallmark of the region and the country. Part of the magic of my little kingdom was that I never even thought about social classes or anything like that; I played soccer with other kids and enjoyed life as children are supposed to.

I lived in a bubble that sooner or later was going to burst. I was too young to realize that outside the fence there was a civil war that was spreading throughout the country and was about to hit my family for the first time, as it had with thousands of other families.

As guerrillas began to operate in the surrounding areas, they also tried to show force, and the way to do so was to send messages to the government and other companies operating in the region, so they attacked farms and killed all kinds of people, from engineers to farmhands as well as military men. The message became apparent to all: this was war!

To avoid risks, my parents decided to move the family "temporarily" to Bogotá, the capital city. Reluctantly, I left behind some of the best memories I have of my life; I had lost my world, the place I loved and where I wanted to be an entrepreneur and agronomist. My father stayed, but the rest of us had to leave: a displaced family starting all over again in a big city.

Even though we were "lucky" because we had financial means, I became alienated as I was living and studying in a place I did not like, with a new culture. Bogotá seemed to me like another country. Everything was different: the buildings, the weather, and the people. No one greeted anyone. Social classes defined personal relationships.

I became aware of the social classes at school. I didn't like the superficial relationships, the hypocrisy, and lack of empathy for others; it was just too much for me. I felt totally alienated and, quite honestly, I never got used to it. I sought peace in books and became an active reader. I also learned English and German studying at home. I loved philosophy and poetry — the latter became the most effective way to express my feelings.

We lived there for about nine years. My father continued in Urabá, managing his farms, and came to see us once a month. It was very nice to see him although he seemed to grow older faster than normal: his hair began to turn grey even though he was still in his forties. He began to drink more than usual and became irritable. I loved that man, and I knew something was wrong, but he wouldn't tell us what it was. We argued sometimes because I wanted to study agronomy and come back to work with him, but he wouldn't let me. I couldn't understand him; it was my dream and it seemed to gradually become unreachable. We lived all those years fearful that something would happen to my father; we told him to sell the farms and leave, but his profession was his life, and he simply couldn't leave it behind.

My father was an entrepreneur but one of a different sort: he believed companies had a responsibility to the community, so he paid his workers well and did not share the landowners' practice of abusing the people in need (the local peasants) by offering low wages and bad working conditions. This made him unpopular with the right-wing paramilitary groups that operated in the zone as an intimidation force to keep the region under "control." He was not afraid of anyone and carried on with his activism. We knew that sooner or later someone would try to silence him, but we knew he wouldn't give up his convictions or his love for the country.

On the morning of July 6, 1995, my father was shot in the head and killed by a group of paramilitary hitmen right in front of his workers. The terrible news was delivered to us a couple of hours later. Other details only became known to us over a few years of hearings through the testimony of ex-combatants during the legal proceedings.

His death was a heavy blow to the family, and of course for me. I was the oldest son and I had to support my mother and my family. Shortly after his murder we were all forced into exile; I went to Mexico and the rest of my family went to the U.S. We had lost our father, our land, our livelihood, and all of a sudden, I became a displaced young man for the second time, and a poor orphan.

This was the poem I wrote to my father shortly after his death:

Shadows

(from the book "Shadows and Poetry" 2000)

One morning of infernal hues,

With a burning sun and detestable shadows,

you left,

you got lost,

and in the immense plantations that soak up the wickedness of some men,

you vanished.

You left, You got lost,

And when I came back, I couldn't see you,

There were no more butterflies or charms,

And my weeping, I couldn't contain it anymore.

You left

You got lost,

Maybe with part of my happiness, leaving me to fight alone.

You got lost,

I look for you in the children, but I can't find you, I sadly regret the day you departed.

You left,

In a dismal box, so sombre,

where I never wanted to see you.

Maybe,

If one day you think the Earth is worth the trouble, come back to the children, there will be an open crib.

I hope to see you!

I hope to see you!

Maybe we'll play soccer and watch the games on TV!

Maybe we'll play soccer and watch the games on TV!

Nonetheless, those years in Mexico as a young, lonely man were very fruitful. I made many contacts and learned a lot about the real world. My situation was far from easy. Every day after work, I would go alone at night to the terrace of the old building I lived in and look at the magnificent and enormous Mexico City that lay before, longing to return to my country and having the same feeling I had experienced when I was a child looking at those vast banana plantations, and later, the city of Bogotá where I was displaced for the first time. It was the same feeling, no matter where I went. I was just an immigrant who belonged nowhere; I understood that our nationality, our family, our belongings, our sense of stability and wellness are a mere illusion, because we are just fragile bone boxes adrift on this planet, in this life, and in the universe. A displaced person learns that; an immigrant knows it well, though sadly those who live a comfortable life just learn about it when they are on their deathbed, and it is too late. All this attachment makes them lead mostly unhappy lives.

L'immigrant
(original French text)

Par Pedro A. Restrepo
Je suis un immigrant,
une créature d'ici et d'ailleur,
je suis comme l'eau
comme la petite goutte que tombe dans l'étang.

Je suis un étranger,
une âme qui va et vient,
une minuscule vague qui court dans le vent.
Je suis un étranger,
une âme qui va et vient,
une minuscule vague qui court dans le vent.

Je suis un enfant de cette universe
mais je n'ai pas de mére ou de pére,
je serai toujours un immigrant,
une créature sans terre
un orphelin.

The Immigrant

(translation)

I am an immigrant
A creature from here and somewhere else, I am like water
Like the tiny drop that falls in the pond.
A stranger
a free soul that comes and goes,
a minuscule wave that runs on the puff.
an alienated,
without home or country
without blood that runs in the duct.
I am a child of this universe, but I have no mother or father. I will always
be an immigrant, a creature without land
and an orphan.

Almost two years later, I decided to come back to my country and continue with my life. I tried to get back our land or at least find out about the details of what we had left behind. But violence and crime made it impossible for me to come back to Urabá.

When my mother knew what I was trying to do, she feared something bad could happen to me, so she returned to Colombia and convinced me to come to the U.S. with her. Very reluctantly, I accepted and once again I was an alien.

Like all immigrants, I had a hard time at first. I had to do many kinds of jobs and longed to return to my country when I had the chance. I was in the U.S. for almost two years, but every day I dreamed of coming back to Colombia where I wanted to become a writer and start my own company. I tried to hold my breath and went on until the feeling was unbearable and I decided to come back in December 1999. I wrote poetry and that helped me to get my feelings and priorities straight.

Shortly after, I published my first book, *Sombras y Poesía* (*Shadows and Poetry*), as a tribute to the two most important men in my life: my father and my grandfather.

In Colombia, I worked as a translator, interpreter, and teacher, and after many years I grew my company and expanded it. I also met and married a wonderful woman and we have been together for fourteen years. Together we built a prosperous business, which at one point had sixteen employees. It made me very happy because I had followed in my father's footsteps, becoming an entrepreneur like him. It was not in the kind of business I had dreamed of as a child, but I felt he would be as proud of me as I was of myself.

Although life was nice, Colombia still suffered with social problems, corruption, and crime. Every time we left home, we feared we might not make it back. Colombians learn to live with such uncertainty, as life means nothing to many.

My aunt was killed in 2002 while she travelled with her family on a rural road. In this case, the violence was from a left-wing group called FARC. She had refused to be kidnapped and did not stop the car when they told her to. Her crime was being a hard-working citizen who had succeeded in her job; in Colombia, that is grounds for a death sentence to criminal groups who are always trying to finance their activities by kidnapping and extorting or stealing property from its lawful owners.

After eighteen years of hard work, my business was doing well, which gave me time to write, and to be a journalist for a magazine that focussed on entrepreneurship. I received local recognition for my work as a poet and storyteller with several publications launched in public libraries, as well as national recognition by the Colombian Ministry of Education as a professional in literature and art, granted in 2002 after a contest in which authors from all over the country submitted their works.

In late 2017, we faced extortion from right-wing paramilitaries, and my wife and I were forced by the circumstances to leave the country again in 2018. I came to Canada and studied international business management and became a professional interpreter at Humber College.

Although it was difficult and painful to leave everything behind and become displaced once again, it was a lot easier to "swallow the pill" this time, as Canada embraced us with open arms and gave us the opportunity to start again and make our dreams come true. I had to learn to be adaptable, flexible, and unattached, and to take prosperity as a temporary gift, knowing it might not last forever and that my life is not the past or the future, but my present.

Luckily for us, we had the chance to heal our wounds and land in this wonderful country where justice really works, and hard-working people can thrive. A place whose government and culture supports human rights and goodness, and actually promotes them. The true land of the free, the only place where the snowy mountains are warmer than the tropical fire, my new home, Canada.

Our lives are full of events and experiences. Some are pleasant, others not so much. When a family suffers a loss due to murder, the tendency is to hate and seek revenge which, in turn, takes the family into a spiral of violence and suffering. Others become permanent victims, suffering more spiritual damage than the actual loss, causing people to be stuck in time. It affects their ability to move forward.

What happens around us is not always in our hands, nor is it even our choice. If we have to face displacement, crime, violence, or threats, we shouldn't let that make us bitter, unhappy, or vengeful. Often our executioners are, were, or have been victims themselves.

Let us move forward and strive to make the world a better place for all.

Canada

(Excerpt from the book *Scars and Hope*, 2022)

Land like no other,
where the snow feels so warm,
where the cold stones laid on the path, are hotter than the tropical fire.
Land where the selfish cannot reign, where life and happiness,
Are worth a gold vein.
Realm of stillness and peace, where its creatures dare not to be
vicious,
to be unhappy, materialistic, or mean.
Icy kingdom

where men walk free to dream and love,
to share without greed.
    Oh! fragile Paradise that we are entrusted to keep!! Sweet and tough
    to the core,
We are the people,
We are the North!

Ilamaran "Maran" Nagarasa and Dishaly Ilamaran
(Sri Lanka)

ILAMARAN NAGARASA, known as Maran, is a freelance journalist, human rights activist, and refugee advocate who lives with his family in Toronto. Originally from Sri Lanka, Maran arrived in Canada in 2009 after travelling with seventy-five other refugees on the boat *Ocean Lady*. He, along with many others, was arrested on suspicion of being a Tamil terrorist and was imprisoned for months without charges before his release. After seven years of struggle with immigration bureaucracy, he was finally allowed to bring his young family to Canada. Over the past twenty years, Maran has been active in reporting human rights abuses in Sri Lanka, including providing testimony at the United Nations Human Rights Commission in 2015. He currently works for a Toronto-based multicultural radio and television company as a news editor.

DISHALY ILAMARAN is a dedicated student at Carleton University, pursuing a dual degree in Journalism and Law. Hailing from Canada since 2016, she is the daughter of Ilamaran Nagarasa. With a passion for storytelling and legal advocacy, Dishaly is committed to weaving together her cultural roots and academic pursuits in her journey of learning and growth.

Maran's Unknown Journey

LIFE IS AN unknown map. From birth to death, each step made is a destination discovered by the individual. I have travelled places I never expected to. I chose a path, not knowing the beginning, middle, or end. I have been brought here by the faith I have in myself and by the promise I made to succeed in my journey. Tamil is my language and identity. It is one of the oldest living languages in this world. It has a beautiful culture, art, and history. I grew up learning the importance of discipline, culture, and duty. These were among the teachings my mother set out for her children to help them undergo the trials of this world.

The love from my neighbourhood was pure. The surroundings and nature I grew up in were ordinary, but the air I breathed was not pleasant. As my knowledge expanded from birth, I realized the danger that surrounded me. Later on, I became aware of the structural genocide occurring to my people, Tamils. We were forced to live in a violent environment. I decided to join members of my community whose goal is to bring permanent peace to our country. I accepted this duty with no second thought. To have our freedom and rights. To live without fear. I tried my hardest in every possible way. But in the end, more than 140,000 Tamil men, women, and children were massacred in the war with no mercy in May 2009.

That month was a black hole in Tamil history. Most of the victims had no clue as to why they were murdered. This was racial oppression. The Sri Lankan government does not value human life. They didn't allow any international people to monitor the war. Tamils begged the United Nations officials, who were located in the northern part of Sri Lanka, where the war occurred, to not leave them. Their cries were "Don't leave us as orphans." Yet those cries were not heard. Years went by before, during an interview on *Sri Lanka's Killing Fields*, broadcast by the British TV station Channel 4, Gordon Weiss, former United Nation spokesman in Sri Lanka, said "It was a mistake."

Twelve years have passed, yet no justice has been served for the lost souls. The war's victims have been urging the international bodies to launch a war crime investigation and to find their lost loved ones, yet no progress has been made. I testified at the United Nations Human Rights Council in Geneva, twice, as a living witness that the Tamil genocide happened. At this point, I am thinking back to the war victim's question, "Has the United Nation Human Rights system been politicized?"

Leaving my motherland, Sri Lanka, to escape death threats, I flew to Thailand in July 2009 and entered an unknown place, holding on to that hope of sailing far away into the hands of a safer country. It was the beginning of my true journey.

One of the struggles I faced was when the traffickers put me and twenty other refugees on a fishing trawler. After twenty-four hours of cruising, we were transferred to a small cargo ship at midnight. For six weeks, I was trapped in the middle of the ocean with seventy-five other men. The ordeal tested each of our limits, both physically and emotionally. In the beginning, we all were lost in our thoughts, disconnected from each other by our fears, trying to run away from our past yet concerned for our uncertain future. I nearly lost all my hope, questioning my decisions. I wondered if I had made the right choice for the sake of my daughter, my wife, and my family. Day and night I was lost within myself. I couldn't swim, yet there I was, sailing on the ocean, with no training or knowledge whatsoever.

One night we faced a huge storm. It wasn't the first — there had been seven other storms before it — but it was the biggest. We hid under the deck to avoid being thrown off the boat and into the water. We feared for our lives. I snuck up, joining with the others as they all peered out into the sea. Pure silence, each of us lost in our world. I wondered, "What awaits us? Will we make it alive? Am I going to be able to see those beautiful smiles from my wife and daughter? What are they doing? I hope they're okay." The sea's expanse unsettled me, its terrifying strength and power to end our lives frightened me. I felt like we were playing with death itself.

One night, looking out at the ocean, watching the water, listening to the sound of waves crashing together, I lost the will to live. Right then and there I wanted to jump into the ocean and become part of it. I wanted to forget everything else. But I didn't. Instead, I lived for the rest of us.

Some nights, the sound of sea waves was like a lullaby, and the ship resembled a cradle, rocking back and forth, helping us all fall asleep peacefully. There were days when hundreds of joyful dolphins would pass by. Sea birds and flying fish flew past and over the ship. These became beautiful memories I can never forget. They made us forget the sadness, and gave meaning to this adventure we were experiencing.

Watching the men, knowing they were thinking the same things I was, I realized that I still had a role to play. Each of their faces held an expression; their trauma, their distress, and the ache for what they had left behind were all etched into their features. As a human being, I felt a need to assist them to share their stories and get each other to open up. I hoped we could all come together and work for however long we needed until we reached land, even if there was no land as far as our eyes could see.

At first, some were very suspicious of my actions. I put myself in their positions; they must be wondering, "Who is this man? Why does he want to know? Can I trust him?" Others were not so suspicious. Some knew who I was, what I did, and what my goals were.

I started by sharing my story, elaborating on my work as a journalist: the things I had witnessed while recording and reporting, the cruelties of what had been done to one community — Tamils — by the government, and what they've done to the media. The threats my family and I faced because of my reporting to the world about the human rights violations by the Sri Lankan government. How thoughts of my family — my hope that they were safe — kept me on edge throughout this journey. Questioning every decision I had made to get to that moment.

I wanted to cry. Talking about my family brought back memories and reminded me of how much I missed them. But I stayed strong for the sake of myself and others. One by one, every one of them started opening up. In the end, I comforted them with a promise that they would be reunited with their loved ones one day. We held hands and prayed together. Christians and Hindus repeated each other's creeds and danced to the improvised music performed with cups and cutlery. We were lost in each other's moment of happiness, forgetting the storm, the ocean, our past. No religion is higher than humanity. At last, that night, we felt like we were at home. It was an astounding feeling; one I hadn't felt in weeks.

Days turned into weeks, weeks into months. Then, one day at dusk, we spotted an airplane with a maple leaf on it. None of us could believe that we had reached Canadian waters. At last, after all those days, our ship, the infamous MV *Ocean Lady* with its seventy-six Tamils, was nearing land. There are no words to describe the joy and excitement we felt.

The Canadian Coast Guard intercepted the vessel off the coast of Vancouver Island. We ran out from under the deck, jumped up and down, threw our fists in the air in joy, and waved our hands calling for help, to be seen and rescued. After forty-five days, I felt relieved. I felt hope that, at last, I'd be able to do something and be with my family again. And I also wanted to fulfill my promise to help everyone else reunite with their loved ones. Following after the Canadian navy ship, I slept peacefully that night.

However, when I woke up the next morning, there were guns pointed at me. I thought that we'd returned to Sri Lanka and that the joy had all been a dream. It took me a moment to realize that this was the Canadian military. The hope and joy had come to an end: we were being arrested at gunpoint.

We spent a night at the Victoria prison and then were transferred to a prison in Vancouver where we lived for the next four months. Three of us shared a prison cell. The cell itself contained a bunk bed and an extra floor mattress. We took turns, switching sleeping spots each night. It was like the devil himself was playing games with us, draining all our energy for no reason. But I was glad to not to be in a Sri Lankan prison where prisoners would be tortured till death.

However, the amount of mental torture in the Canadian prison was far worse than I would've expected. I felt safer yet not accepted in this new country. We didn't know what was going on in the outside world. The arrest was something I hadn't expected. I was healthy on the ship, but here in this dark underground, I felt sick. When I looked at my cellmates,

I saw soulless eyes. At least on the ship we'd had the ability to communicate and support one another, and that had given us strength. Each of us were there for one another; we were a family, facing whatever obstacles we came up against. But here, in this dreadful place, we weren't allowed to communicate as much. We watched television and became aware that many in the Canadian media were labelling us "terrorists." I wished to die rather than bear this false title. It was a word the Sri Lankan government wanted the world to use to describe us. Without being aware of it, Canada had succeeded in fulfilling the Sri Lankan government's horrible wish. I wish Canada would have listened to our stories and words before making this false accusation.

I knew I had to have faith that good things would happen at some point. And slowly, bit by bit, things got better for all of us. We were let out of prison, though I felt like a zombie.

Our life in Canada wasn't pleasant at first. Even though we'd been released, it was under conditions something like a house arrest. For almost four and a half years, every week, I had to go to the immigration office in person to report that I was still there. I had a curfew from midnight to six in the morning. I felt like a caged bird with a tracker on my back. This was not the freedom I had hoped for. What was done is done, but I hope this mistake never happens again in Canada.

My bond person, one of my media friends, took me in and treated me with kindness. I spent a whole year under the same roof with his family. Although I missed my own family, I was glad to have made another that'll last a lifetime.

Back in Sri Lanka my wife and daughter were moving from place to place, hiding for their safety due to threats against their lives. Because of this, I had to wait to receive their call. The resulting stress I faced wasn't something everyone understood. Three years went by before my wife and daughter were able to take refuge in India in the middle of 2012. Finally, I was able to talk to them through video calls. It was something, which was better than nothing. Still, I needed to find a way to bring them here, to reunite them with me. I didn't want to keep hearing that dreadful question from my daughter, "When will I get to see you, Dad?" It was a question

I had no answer to, other than "One day, darling." It was so painful whenever Dishaly mentioned wanting to be in my arms, missing those goodnight kisses and hugs. I didn't know when I would be able to fulfill her wish, but I had hope.

Along this journey, I came across PEN Canada members and Mary Jo Leddy, who was the chairperson. My lawyer, a good friend, Andrew Brouwer, was the person to introduce me to them. They were another family I quickly became a part of, and I will be thankful for the rest of my life. They have helped me a lot. And PEN members listened to my refugee hearing. I was accepted as a refugee in May 2013, but it was another three and a half years before I was able to reunite with my family. It wasn't an easy process. The dedication and effort of Mary Jo Leddy, Andrew, and PEN members paid off.

August 2, 2016, was the best day of my life. It was the day I finally reunited with my family. It was the day I was able to hold the two precious women in my life.

A part of my mind was at ease. However, this wasn't the end. I've been helping the rest of the men I arrived with to reunite with their families. We've grown closer. Nowadays, we rarely allow our non-secular differences to result in hatred and conflict. Fourteen years have gone by, and still some families haven't been able to have the happiness that I'm thankful to have. They don't know when they'll be able to be together with their families. They don't know what will or could happen in their lives. They resemble lifeless corpses walking around with no emotion. I will help them, one way or another. I have to: my promise hasn't been fulfilled yet. This story has yet to see its end.

Acknowledgements

I WOULD FIRST like to first thank the members of Writers in Exile. From its humble beginnings as a casual supper club hosted by Mary Jo Leddy at Romero House refugee shelter, it has emerged as a big family of multinational writers under the supportive banner of PEN Canada.

For this, our first anthology, I would like to thank the intrepid Arzu Yildiz for introducing me to many of the writers here and suggesting the idea of a book. I'd also like to remember Aaron Berhane, friend, leader of the Writers in Exile group and contributor who passed away from Covid before he saw this anthology realized. And I want to thank our generous editing team of Margo Kelly, Anneli Andre-Barrett, and Hannah Fisher for their work with the writers, not just for the editing of the pieces but for their encouragement of the writers and the mentoring of language and presentation for our reading events at Hirut Ethiopian Jazz Club.

Our agent, Sam Hiyate of The Rights Factory, immediately understood the potential and did a stellar job of marketing this book, and publisher Marc Côté and his team at Cormorant Books offered tremendous enthusiasm from the start.

It has been a privilege and honour to meet these writers and read of their experiences. They have taught me how resilient the human spirit can be, and they have taught me how lucky I am to have been born in one of a shrinking number of countries that recognizes human rights and freedom of the press.

—KRL

We acknowledge the sacred land on which Cormorant Books operates. It has been a site of human activity for 15,000 years. This land is the territory of the Huron-Wendat and Petun First Nations, the Seneca, and most recently, the Mississaugas of the Credit River. The territory was the subject of the Dish With One Spoon Wampum Belt Covenant, an agreement between the Iroquois Confederacy and Confederacy of the Ojibway and allied nations to peaceably share and steward the resources around the Great Lakes. Today, the meeting place of Toronto is still home to many Indigenous people from across Turtle Island. We are grateful to have the opportunity to work in the community, on this territory.

We are also mindful of broken covenants and the need to strive to make right with all our relations.